CW01507093

AGE SHALL
NOT
WEARY THEM

AGE SHALL NOT WEARY THEM

1st Battalion Royal Sussex Regiment

ROY REES

MENIN HOUSE

Tommies Guides

Menin House

13 Hunloke Avenue

Eastbourne

East Sussex

BN22 8UL

www.tommiesguides.co.uk

First published in Great Britain by Menin House Publishers
an imprint of Tommies Guides, 2011

© 2010 Roy Rees

All rights reserved. Apart from any use under UK copyright law no part
of this publication may be reproduced, stored in a retrieval system, or
transmitted, in any form or by any means, without the prior written
permission of the publisher, nor be otherwise circulated in any form of
binding or cover other than that in which it is published and without a
similar condition being imposed on the subsequent publisher.

ISBN 978 0 95634 263 8

Cover design by Tommies Guides
Typeset by Graham Hales, Derby
Printed and bound in Great Britain by CPI Antony Rowe,
Chippenham and Eastbourne

Contents

Preface

I have waited a long enough time before writing of my experiences in World War 11, but I will try now to give an account of the highs and lows of the years 1938 to 1946. This will therefore include some memories of the time leading up to the War and the time just after peace came.

There was an American film released after the War entitled 'The Best Years of Your Life.' This title of course referred to the sacrifices of what should have been the best years in your life – in my case from the age of 19 to 26.

You never get those years back, the years when you were healthy and young. Some never came back, some lie in the stillness of a foreign country. Others were maimed or suffered shellshock; some never recovered.

Some found on their return to the UK that their marriages had broken up in their absence. They had to start life all over again in a country which had been badly bombed and where the economy was ailing.

I still possess letters which I wrote to my parents and which they kept; also I still have wartime notes and photographs which I will use to give a true picture of life as it was in the infantry in those days. It will remind us all that nearly 71 years ago the last World War took place.

It is a sobering thought, particularly for those of my age.

A donation from all books sold will go to the Royal Sussex Regimental Association.

CHAPTER 1

Peace and Happiness in the Early Thirties

It is fair to say that in the early thirties my life was certainly a happy one. Our family consisted of our parents and an elder sister and brother, and myself. My brother Ronnie was only one year and seven months older than me. Our sister Edna was the eldest of the siblings, but we were all supportive of one another.

In earlier years my Father had founded a ship broking firm in Swansea and this became a partnership between him and our uncle Tom Stockwood. The business side did well and my father was President of the Swansea Chamber of Commerce for several years.

Our house was quite pleasant, and from it you could view the sea.

I think that in those days my sense of navigation was probably not very good. For occasional treats we were taken on the paddle steamer from Swansea to Ilfracombe and on one occasion after landing at Ilfracombe I had wandered off on my own. I became absorbed in the streets near at hand, and a somewhat irate parent managed to locate me so that we returned to the steamer just in time before it sailed back to Swansea.

On another occasion Ronnie and I were taken by our father in a cargo vessel to a French port. Again I wandered off with my small Brownie camera, and took a few photos of French ships which were naval ones. A gendarme suddenly exploded in front of me with a torrent of French. My father heard the rumpus, and with his knowledge of French he managed to pacify matters, but only after I had given up the film from my camera. An early example I daresay, of the beginning of pre-war security measures.

Not long before leaving my Prep School the slump descended on industry and this had a very adverse effect on trade in South Wales. Ronnie was already at College and Pa said to me one day that if I wanted to join Ronnie at College in Shropshire I would have to get a scholarship. This meant a slog particularly at the Classics, but I had good teachers.

I rushed home one summer day to tell the family the good news that I had obtained a scholarship to Ellesmere College. In fact it was an anti-climax as one of the masters had already phoned my father at his office with the news.

This reminded me of the time a few months earlier when we had played a football match against nearby Bryntirion School. They usually won against us. On this particular occasion we actually won and I was anxious to tell my father and grandfather the good news. When I joined them for tea at the grandparent's house they were much absorbed in a discussion about the serious state of the shipping trade. I daren't interrupt. Eventually my father turned to me and asked, "What have you been up to today?"

"At last we have beaten Bryntirion at football. One nil and I scored the goal," I had managed to get the news out at last. For some happy moments the state of the economy was forgotten.

And so eventually I left Craig-y-nos School in Swansea to start my years at Ellesmere College in Shropshire where Ronnie, as forerunner, was very helpful to me as I learned the ropes, and guiding me with such helpful advice. We were both now in Woodard House.

Certainly those years away from home were quite Spartan. Apart from the living conditions which were quite basic, it could be bitterly cold in that region, so when the opportunity occurred we huddled around the basic radiators in the vast halls. I mention this as it meant that when the war started we were already inured to such a life away from home.

When reaching the VIth Form one was able to concentrate on certain subjects, and, although the only Universities around to consider in those days were Oxford and Cambridge, I felt that perhaps I could carry on in that direction. However I owed a greater debt to my parents at this time of economic downturn, and I resolved to join Ronnie in London in order to carve out a future if that were possible in the Big City.

Whilst at Ellesmere there was a work ethos instilled into one and there was also a strong Christian tradition as we were one of the Woodard Foundation Schools. The attendances at Chapel were strictly adhered to. Leisure time was enjoyable, with rugby, cricket and tennis, also swimming and golf. Those with good voices soon found a place in the choir. You could also progress from the Scouts to the Cadets, but in those peaceful days I had little interest in the latter.

I never considered that an acting career was in my stars. I remember that in the annual Shakespeare play of Macbeth I played the part of Young Siward. My role in the later stages of the play was to come on stage and make bold noises to Macbeth about my father's death (the elder Siward). The sword play between myself and Macbeth (the beefy Headmaster) was a one-sided affair, and before acting as 'dead' I heard someone in the audience shout, "Come on young 'un."

I did however, take part in a play in Latin concerning a card game. At one stage in this play I had to throw down my cards in anger, but even that would not have been of help with any Thespian desire anyway.

In some cases one made friends at Ellesmere that lasted for life, and in one of the summer holidays not long before the war, Ronnie and I went camping in Devon with two friends from Ellesmere. The area we chose was near Lynton and Lynmouth; the names of the friends were Rigby and Lewis, who were in fact in a different House. They were peaceful days indeed. Another friend at Ellesmere was Ian Shepherd[1] whose forte was in music and choral work

Eventually when I left Ellesmere I joined Ronnie in London where he was already working with a bank. I joined the Head Office of an Insurance Company. We had 'digs' in Lewisham and our landlady was a Mrs. Poole. She was a widow who had lost her organist husband, and she became a good friend to us. The office where I worked was situated on the Victoria Embankment and they had a sports ground in Kent.

---

1 Ian Shepherd has now sadly passed away

I can remember a Bank Holiday outing with Ronnie when we went to the peaceful Kentish countryside. On another Bank Holiday I ventured as far as Hampton Court, where by chance I came across an old school friend by the name of Hawkins. He was with some of his family up from Cornwall. They invited me to share tea with them. Later that week I went with Hawkins to see the Music Hall at Shepherds Bush Empire where Max Miller was performing. We also visited a pleasant hostelry on the river-front. It was too peaceful even to think of war. We had both been in the School Eleven at cricket and we recalled games now long past.

The seasons changed and one evening after a game of rugby for the office, two friends by the name of Miller and Everitt came over to chat with me near the bar. Clearly they thought that I was a suitable candidate to join the Territorial Army, especially as there was a shadow over dealings with Germany. The annexation of territory had become serious, and these two chaps had already joined The Queen's Westminsters, a Territorial Unit of the King's Royal Rifle Corps. (KRRC).

At College I had never shown much interest in the Cadet Force, but it seemed at this time in the winter of 1938 that the more young men who joined the voluntary arms of the Services the better; perhaps it could have an effect on the thinking of the Germans.

So I duly joined up in the Queen's Westminsters, but my two colleagues from the office were already in the First Battalion which now had a full complement, so I landed in the Second Battalion. In the Second Battalion we had a Platoon of famous names in the theatrical world including, Frank Lawton, Nigel Patrick, Jimmy Hanley and Guy Middleton.

During the summer of 1939 I duly joined my Battalion for summer camp in the New Forest. It rained heavily most of the time and there were plenty of adders to watch out for as well! A few exercises were held and my tent companions seemed to be Cockney types who accepted me into their group with goodwill.

After a fortnight I returned to my digs in London and I can remember saying to Mrs. Poole, "Thank God that's over for another year, we were like drenched rats." Of course I was ultimately wrong; it was not over for another year in fact.

Exams at work were going quite well, and for a holiday I had been asked by two contempories to join them for a holiday on the Norfolk Broads. These two were colleagues in the office, namely Alan Slater who had joined the Artists Rifles and Miller who had persuaded me to join the Queen's Westminsters.

However, my parents wanted me home for this holiday, and looking back at it all they were no doubt fairly sure that war was looming.

Even so, I carried on playing cricket for the office at weekends, and in late summer the office sports ground seemed a peaceful haven. And then the office Rugby Club including myself, carried out a sandbagging operation on Hamilton House, our office headquarters on Victoria Embankment overlooking the Thames. It was hot work in that August weather. You could rely on the seasons in those days. People began to feel resigned to war, but as long as Hitler refrained from attacking Poland there was still a chance of 'Peace in our Time.'

In the week before the outbreak of war, Ronnie was called up to his Regiment, the Royal Fusiliers, and in my case the call up was carried out alphabetically, so the week was nearly over before I reported to Buckingham Gate in London.

I can remember so well the sincere handshakes I received in the office, especially from those who had been in the First World War. No doubt they still remembered the horrors of the trenches in their own time and they hoped it would not be so bad for us. On the Saturday evening, when the Battalion was assembled in the Buckingham Gate area, the heavens opened and the thunder and lightning rolled across London and our meagre billets. Premonitions perhaps of what was to come? A warning from the Gods, a warning of Armageddon perhaps.

By Sunday morning the weather had cleared somewhat and we marched up to St. James Church in Piccadilly for the Sunday service. During the service the voice of Neville Chamberlain came over the air. There had been no reply to the Governments ultimatum regarding Poland, and a state of war now existed with Germany.

We were beginning to troop out of the church when all of a sudden the air raid sirens started wailing. We were told to make ready our gas masks. How vulnerable and ill prepared we were. Our rifles were old American ones, and some time elapsed before we were issued with the reliable Lee Enfields. With winter approaching it seemed as if we might have to face up to the colder weather, not with greatcoats but the present issue of busmen's overcoats.

On that first occasion of the sirens blasting off the world seemed to go silent, but no enemy planes appeared. Possibly it had been a reconnaissance plane of some sort. Certainly from now on our lives would never be the same again.

The Second World War had started with the German invasion of Poland, and we wondered what the future held for us, and what our immediate tasks would be.

7 Gilmore Rd
S.E. 13.

Sept 4. 1939

Dear Mr & Mrs Rees,

I thank you for your letter of tonight. Roy went very bravely on Saturday and I gave him 3 stamped envelopes and paper to let you know he had arrived but up to now he has not had time unless he can to-night. The lady who resides at the next house here, her

Copy of correspondence from Mrs Poole to my parents. Note the date.

husband went a week ago
and up to now not a
word from him, and they
I know would write if at
all possible

It is a great joy to know
that neither of the Boys
are to be sent abroad, so
we read in the papers as
neither when joining were 21.
We miss them very much
and I shall be ever so
glad to hear that they are
well and happy.
Roy had to take food for the
day so I packed him up,
enough food, and my sister who
is staying here with me
added to helping him
She is a regular helper and

I sent Webb (gardener) with
him to the station with
his Kit Bag. to help along.
Yes, Your lads are perfect
and I just felt ill when
the "call up", came.

Let us hope it will soon
be over.
I know how you feel, but
do be proud of them both
said, how glad they were
they came to you on the
Sunday. I am too.

I hope You are all quite
well. As soon as ever I
hear I will post the letter
to Roy at once.

With all wishes that they
will soon return to work,
Yours v. sincerely B. M. Poole

CHAPTER 2

The War of Tasker's Ear

Within a short time we had moved to Willesden Junction for guard duties on what was called a Vulnerable Point (VP). This was an important rail junction on the periphery of London and we were billeted in LMS railway sleepers in a siding. Usually the trains roared through without stopping and some of the guard work was at night. The worst hours to be on sentry duty were between 2 am and 4 am. With those hours you knew that you could only sleep until the small hours before being woken, and by the time you returned to your carriage the night would not last much longer for your delayed rest.

On sentry duties I made other friends including a group from Glynn Mills Bank and a rifleman named Hugh Brown, with whom I kept in touch after the war.

On one occasion some of us were paraded on a quiet platform and we went through the usual drill with our rifles, including a check on clearance of rounds from the barrel. Unfortunately on this particular occasion one rifleman hadn't appreciated that he still had one round that hadn't been cleared, and when he squeezed the trigger in clearance the round was fired. The rifleman next to him had the name of Tasker and the discharged bullet damaged Tasker's ear. The accident could of course been so much worse, and the incident became known as the War of Tasker's Ear. No doubt a take on The War of Jenkin's Ear from past history.

Shortly after this incident we moved to the London Docks for a tour of guard duties. The winter weather was now beginning to bite and for sentry duty in this environment we not only had to wear our normal equipment but also a lifejacket. You had to walk like a penguin and a pregnant one at that. The paths between the deep watery locks were narrow and darkness usually reigned. There was an atmosphere of eeriness.

One night I called out to a foreign docker the usual, "Halt, who goes there?" Very quickly he replied that he was a Japanese sailor, and he quickly added, "And Hitler is a bastard." The Japs were not yet our enemy. We had a certain amount of respite in one of the waterfront warehouses, but we were not sorry to get movement orders again.

This time we set ourselves up in Hampstead with Christmas on the horizon. Our billets this time were a children's school and the toilets were too small for comfort! Unfortunately I was on Mess duty for the Christmas lunch and festivities. Having completed this work I looked forward to the New Year, and I felt confident enough to arrange a date with a lady I knew from office days and who lived in the near area. I suggested that we meet at Golders Green with a view to going to the cinema. Alas, shortly before our date I was put on guard duty for the same night. I tried in vain to get someone to stand in for me on the guard duty, but of course they all wanted to go out for the New Year. No phone was available and the best I could manage was a letter of apology to the lady in question. It made me realise that in wartime we were on duty all the time unless on official leave.

A little later I was given a short leave which I was able to spend with Mrs. Poole at Lewisham. A proper bath at last was heaven sent.

I wonder how we managed on 14 shillings a week, 2 shillings a day, from which we had to find money for laundry and haircuts when necessary.

I was beginning to enjoy the walks on Hampstead Heath and even the marches, especially when Tommy Barton, our Company Commander, started up a favourite song of the day and we all joined in, loudly.

Then all of a sudden, without knowing the cause I contracted scarlet fever. This was a blow to me and I felt quite ill for a time in Grove Hospital, Tooting. I don't suppose I was too popular with the Company as they were put in quarantine for a time. In the first instance I was put in a 3 bed ward with two others, one of whom was a dispatch rider. Then one day when the nurse came in she spoke to me in kindly words, "Come on Arthur, you are well enough to make your own bed now." The other two patients looked at me quizzically as they had known me as Roy. They were somewhat amused at this, and then I realised that the nurse was reading off the details at the foot of my bed. My first mane was Arthur but I was always known as Roy, my second name. My father and Mrs. Poole managed to come and see me in hospital, suitably attired in white smocks. This was very kind of them.

A short time later there was a reorganisation of the wards, and the three of us found ourselves in a large ward where about a dozen beds were filled. The withdrawal from Dunkirk was the reason for this and I watched as the poor wounded French and Belgian soldiers were taken to their allotted wards. The war had come nearer to us all.

Unfortunately in those days with scarlet fever one usually contracted complications and in my case there were ear problems. This prolonged my stay in hospital, and it took quite a while before it cleared up.

On one occasion I was walking on the grass outside the ward where there was a swing. One of the nurses whom I had befriended came along and I gave her a push on the swing which she quite enjoyed. Unfortunately, Matron observed my antics and she was not best pleased.

For all that the discipline was really effective, with light relief at times. Usually first thing in the morning a good old fashioned char by the name of Maud polished and polished the wooden floor, and at the same time was chirpy to all of us.

Eventually I was discharged from hospital as the ear problem had sufficiently cleared up.

CHAPTER 3

Autumn 1940 to March 1941

I rejoined the Queen's Westminsters and my former friends gave me a hearty welcome back. At the beginning of September in 1940, we were posted to St. Donat's Castle in Llantwit Major in Glamorgan in South Wales. This was good news for me to be back in the Principality, and we had our tented camp in the Castle grounds near the sea. The Officers were billeted in the Castle itself, and I can recall that Evelyn Laye, who was married to Frank Lawton, entertained the Battalion with her professionalism.

The war had now been on for a year, and we were gradually becoming hardened to the way of life.

In the early part of September we took part in a Brigade exercise. This involved our battalion and the London Rifle Brigade attacking Rhossilli Bay which was held by the London Scots. In particular, our unit had to take Llanmadoc Hill from Cheriton. These places were all over the Gower Peninsular, west of Swansea, which my family knew so well. Llanmadoc Hill was quite a hill to climb.

It was of course, somewhat unfortunate to say the least, as we motored past the flats in Swansea where my parents lived. I was unable to stop, and to make matters worse on the return journey the road gave way beneath our bus. This was at 10 o'clock at night and we were under the bridge by the LMS station in Swansea. We could not go on and we were stuck for about two hours before a reserve bus picked us up. During this time the air-raid sirens sounded off and gave the all clear at the same time! Then later, the sirens went off again and the searchlights played again. The naval 12 pounders then went into action. Swansea certainly endured a rough time with the bombing. The Germans were beginning to realise the importance of Swansea Docks, and it was sometime later before the air defences were adequate. From the war point of view the German planes missed the docks, but sadly they took out some famous landmarks in the town centre. It had been a 24 hour exercise. We did not return to our camp until 5 o'clock in the morning, having been on the go all day and night.

It was whilst we were at St. Donat's Castle near Llantwit Major that the church bells throughout the land rang out one day. Had something happened on the East Coast of England? There was an eerie quietness except for the lap of waves on the sea near by. Eventually we all stood down. Was it ever really explained properly?

My father motored up from Swansea one Sunday to see me, and we took some of my friends to tea at a local hotel.

Our Battalion also had to stay at Crickhowell near Abergavenny. We were billeted in Nissen huts in Crickhowell Park. The Signals Officer was a Lieutenant Kaiser who encouraged Hugh Brown and myself to learn Morse code and Semaphore. We quite enjoyed this challenging task.

In our Nissen hut in Crickhowell one day I was having a warm by the stove, and I did not realise that my new greatcoat was getting burnt! When I realised what had happened I felt distraught. I couldn't hide the damage. This was where my friends came into their own. I did not ask any questions but they managed to get me a new greatcoat and all was well again. You never forget these kindnesses.

In December 1940 we moved to Keele Hall near Newcastle-under-Lyme in Staffordshire. I remember on one occasion I was sitting at the end of the table at lunch when the Officer came round to ask if there were any complaints. I realised the Officer was Frank Lawton. There were no complaints but he showed an interest in our food!

It was at this time that I was selected to be one of the ceremonial guard of three riflemen and an NCO. Apparently a bigwig was going to arrive within a few days. I should explain that recently I had helped a rifleman or two to write a letter to their sweethearts or whoever. They needed help with their letter writing, and without knowing the recipients of these letters I gave what help I could. These friends had not forgotten my assistance in this regard, and they were quite determined now that I would be well turned out for this special guard. They certainly helped to spruce up my equipment, and Major Dobbs, our Company Commander at the time, was very concerned that everything would be well on the day.

As the posh car with the Union Jack flag approached we received the order, 'Guard turn out.' This meant that on the icy stonework square we had to double out of the guardroom together with the bugler. The important personage was General Sir John Dill, the Commander of the Imperial General Staff. Fortunately I didn't slip on the ice with ammunition boots on. We presented arms and the CIGS congratulated us on our smartness and spoke to each one of us.

Shortly after this I became a Lance Corporal, and I was recommended for an OCTU course (Officer Cadet Training Unit). At this time in 1941 I was worried for my family as Swansea had undergone a blitz from the air. The seaport stood up to this air attack with great fortitude. I see from my letters that also at this time I was granted 24 hours leave, so I went to Chester. I had bed and breakfast there at TOC.H for half a crown, and it was great value.

Our regiment moved to Scarborough in early March and the Yorkshire Moors provided suitable terrain for exercises. The cafes seemed able to provide very good meals amidst the sea air. We were billeted in a hotel on the seafront.

After interviews at Western Command I was advised that shortly I would be on my way to an OCTU. My Platoon Commander at the time was Bill Deedes, a name that now resonates with his later high office in Government and his achievements in the journalistic world. In the Army he was awarded the MC during the war, and at the time in Scarborough he gave me some useful tips for OCTU including points on navigation. He was an Officer who cared.

My friend Hugh Brown was later to become an Officer when he was a little older.

I had mixed feelings when I bade farewell to the friends I had made in the Queen's Westminsters. I'm sure we had now become more seasoned soldiers, and the Royal Sussex intake had done well alongside us. We shall come across this famous Regiment again eventually.

I felt sad at leaving all my friends as I faced up to the challenges ahead.

CHAPTER 4

OCTU March 1941 – July 1941

There was a very heavy air raid on Scarborough before I left there; the bombing was indiscriminate. Shortly before I entrained for Barmouth on the North Wales coast, the Colonel shook hands with me and wished me the best of luck. And so I made my solitary way from Scarborough to Barmouth. I had a very heavy kitbag with me and the train journey involved changes at Leeds, Manchester, Chester and Ruabon. At Ruabon there was a three hour wait. It was certainly an out of the way place.

Eventually I reached Barmouth and the coast on the other side of Great Britain. My quarters were in the Barmouth Hotel near the seafront and there were still some civilians living in the Hotel. I was to share a bedroom with two other cadets, one from the Royal West Kents and one from Intelligence. The room was a little cramped for three, but overall it seemed a reasonable billet. Our food was also to be served there as well.

The training programme was quite full over the next few months, and the starting programme consisted of drill exercises on the seafront square and lectures. Some sport was included on

Wednesday afternoons and Saturdays, and on Sundays we had a free day. On our battledress uniform we had to wear a white band around the cap, also a red strip on the right shoulder and a white strip on the left shoulder. The red indicated that we were infantry and the white, an OCTU.

Individually we had to control drill periods and weapon training, and there were plenty of field exercises. One of these exercises was carried out at night and involved Barmouth Station. This was in fact, the station that was used in the making of the film called 'The Ghost Train.' It certainly seemed ghostly and deserted when we used it in the exercise. We also had plenty of lectures including military law which I found interesting.

Apart from the sea, some of the terrain was quite mountain-ous and rainy times in Wales were not surprising. Eventually we had finished with March and April, and then May brought some softening of the weather conditions.

Although we were somewhat isolated geographically, the continuance of the war never left our minds. The country was still virtually alone, and apart from the Commonwealth, other powers still had not entered the fray.

In early June my mother was able to visit Barmouth and the families of the other cadets did the same. My mother lived in the midst of Swansea when they had the severe air raids, and we felt that the change would do her good. Although we had little free time, my mother's sojourn worked out quite well. She knew the area, as when we were young our parents took us to Barmouth and Fairbourne for a holiday. Her return journey to Swansea was not too bad either.

By this time I had become more acquainted with the two

chaps sharing the same billets as myself, and they were very pleasant in all ways.

One episode was with a fellow cadet named Flower. I had noticed him on our drill parades as he seemed taller than most. Anyway, one day we took out a small rowing boat and indulged in some local fishing with crude tackle. I'm afraid we were not successful, but the expedition in free time did us good. His surname was to crop up later in the war.

Towards the end of the course we did an extended exercise which entailed climbing to the top of Mount Cader Idris. The weather had dried up by then and the climb up in a supposed war situation was exhilarating. Mountain warfare became realistic for me later on as we shall see, but on that occasion, as the exercise ended I felt at peace with the mountainous terrain and the sky above.

The twelfth week eventually arrived, which was a worrying time for us all, as we knew that the results had gone in to the War Office. Subsequently I learnt that I had obtained a 'good average'; but there were a few who didn't make it, at least not that time around.

Meanwhile I had to fill in preference forms for Regiments and my first choice was for Ox and Bucks Light Infantry. As I had spent earlier days with the Queen's Westminsters who at that time marched at a quick pace as part of KRRC (subsequently they were mechanised), the Light Infantry also marched at a quick pace. Apparently a few Queen's Westminsters had ended up in the Ox and Bucks, but I was content to join the Kings Shropshire Light Infantry, (KSLI), especially as my college days at Ellesmere had been in Salop. Incidentally, at the time the Royal Sussex Regiment was my third choice, and we shall come across them later in this narrative.

It may surprise the reader that I did not include a Welsh Regiment in this list, but they were heavy infantry, whereas the Light Infantry marched faster and there were differences in drill as well. Anyway, before I joined the KSLI at their depot in Shrewsbury I was given a week's leave to spend with my family in Swansea.

The course had ended in early July. On the world stage we were no longer alone; Germany had attacked Russia, so the latter major power became an important ally, to say the least.

CHAPTER 5

Life with the KSLI in Shropshire and in the South East of England

In the third week of July 1941, I reported to Copthorne Barracks, the KSLI Depot in Shrewsbury. The barracks were only a 5 minute walk from the centre of the town. I settled down quickly at the Depot and I was given a pleasant welcome.

Without wasting any time I was soon made Orderly Officer. Also there had recently been an intake of approximately 250 recruits, and I was given the responsibility for training two of these platoons. The CO interviewed me but he could not say how long I would be there. Apparently it all depended on the War Office.

Good news from home included the fact that my brother Ron had also become an Officer, albeit in the Indian Army. He had already distinguished himself by winning a boxing tournament on his ship going to India.

In some ways it was difficult to realise that there was a war on in Shrewsbury. Cricket was often played within the grounds of the Depot, and I can remember walking on the banks of the River

Severn and watching the budding oarsmen of Shrewsbury School practising their sporting ability. The late summer sun was playing peacefully on the river as I watched from shady trees. Perhaps I ought to have gone over to Ellesmere College; however, travel would not have been easy just then.

Anyway, I had an important date coming up on the 24th of July; my 21st birthday. If I had been at the Depot any length of time I've no doubt that I could have celebrated the day with a few others, but I hardly knew them. Also, I owed it to my parents to try and phone them on the day, especially as they could not phone me. I resolved to go into Shrewsbury on the day in question and I managed to phone through to my parents from a large cinema/restaurant building. All was well with the family so I treated myself to a reasonable restaurant meal.

It so happened that shortly after my birthday the Padre told me that a local family would be pleased to play host to someone from the Depot, and he wondered if I would be interested. At first I wasn't all that keen but I agreed to contact them. The family consisted of the parents, and a son and daughter; they had a comfortable house in Shrewsbury. The garden led steeply down to a small stream at the bottom. Unfortunately I cannot remember their names now, but they were very hospitable, and the son was at Shrewsbury School.

Part of my time at the Depot was taken up in the company of an Officer who had apparently blotted his copybook in some way. He had to have an Officer supervising his isolation at this time. I knew virtually nothing about his case; sometimes I would take him round the cricket field boundary. He did not seem to be too put out by his ordeal, and I don't know what became of him eventually.

Life in the Army here was a contrast really to my earlier experiences, and no doubt one could live here if it turned out that way, but I knew in my mind that having put in all the training for war, I needed to branch out to a more sensitive area.

Eventually I received a posting to the 5th Battalion of the KSLI who were based in Sussex at that time. I joined 'A' Company of this Battalion in September 1941. The Company was commanded by Major Bob Gill and two of his officers at that time were Peter Tyrell and Circus, who not unnaturally had the nickname of Bertram. Certainly Bob Gill was one of the best Company Commanders that I came across in those days. I can remember helping with my Platoon to increase the defences of Ford Aerodrome. This entailed having to move a large quantity of barbed wire across the main railway line. Accidents could have happened with this work, and we had to ensure that the barbed wire did not come into contact with the live rail. After the day's work we would march back to our billets in the Yapton area, the march being accompanied by strong singing voices.

Shortly after this posting, I was detailed to take part in one of the biggest exercises, if not the biggest, for a whole week. My Battalion was not taking part, but I was to be an umpire. Firstly I was sent to Tilehurst Camp near Reading, (a home of the Royal Berkshire Regiment). There were about 16 umpires in all and I had arrived there with a personal utility truck and a motor-cycle dispatch rider. From here I was liable to be sent anywhere where the arranged battle might take place. Those taking part were armoured divisions, infantry divisions, artillery and engineers, the RAF and chemical warfare units. I was allotted a sum of money for eventualities which might involve myself, the driver and dispatch rider. We had to try and return to Tilehurst Camp every night where I had my bed in the NAAFI. The exercise was due to end on October 3rd, and I would be allowed to take weekend leave from 3rd to 5th of October. I intended to go up to London for the weekend and see Mrs. Poole again.

On this large exercise I had the task of dashing off to towns and render road junctions cratered by bombs. This of course, meant that large military convoys had to deviate. On these occasions I had a Section of Army Police Traffic Control who helped with the traffic. Meanwhile I had to set off thunderflashes to represent bombs.

The RAF were in as well on what must have been the biggest exercise ever carried out in the UK. At the end of it, I had to destroy all the secret papers which I had been given for the exercise.

After all this I was glad to see Mrs. Poole again, especially as it happened to be her birthday. She kindly treated me to a show at the Victoria Palace called 'Black Vanities.' Afterwards we had dinner at the Regent Palace Hotel.

Eventually our Battalion moved to Dorset, and Sherborne became our base. I was fortunate to be billeted in the Castle, and I was put in charge of the Bren Gun Carrier Platoon. The Carriers were stationed at the top of the hill near the main street. During one period at Sherborne night was turned into make believe day for us and the same applied to all exercises during this period.

It was because of this that the Battalion practiced night convoy movements and the Carrier Platoon had to lead the vehicles on these cold nights. It must be remembered that during those years of threatened invasion all the road signs had been taken down, and usually I was able to reconnoitre the chosen route in daylight hours. However, there was one occasion when I received the route details at a time too late to do a dummy run first. The freezing night came and we led the convoy quite well for a time. But eventually we reached one country road where there was a choice of two lanes in order to make progress. It so happened that I chose the wrong lane and we in the Carriers ended up in a cemetery. As the Carriers were tracked vehicles we were soon able to turn around and correct our mistake. However all the following lorries ended up in a dreadful melee at the lane end.

It was probably about 1am when I finally retired to bed, and sleep was not easy as I anticipated a 'rocket' the following morning. But before morning there was a knock on the door and a Captain Gwynne came in. Whilst he mentioned the navigational error I had made he was more concerned and angry that the lorries had been following me willy-nilly, without checking the route with their maps. So I was let off really, but I did remember how some time ago Bill Deedes had emphasised the importance of navigation to me!

The cold weather continued into February and working on the Carriers at the top of the hill entailed bitter conditions. One day I was told to give instructions to the local police on firing rifles, and also in the art of unarmed combat. For the latter I had a well built sergeant to assist me! At the same time we did manage to have a pleasant social life both in the Castle and in Sherborne itself, and the local residents were very helpful and friendly.

But then I was sent on a course which sounds very mundane, but it turned out to be an unforgettable experience for myself.

CHAPTER 6

Staying the Course

Later on in February 1942, I was sent on a course near Swanage in Dorset. Apparently this was to be the first of what was to become known as 'Battle Courses.' Monty it seemed, thought that the Division needed more hardening up. Nowadays such courses are quite commonplace e, but I could sense we were going to be put through our paces to see what the human frame could stand in bleak wintry conditions.

The course turned out to be so severe that I can only say that at times we were up to our necks in water or climbing over barbed wire or jumping from heights and running, nearly all the time with full equipment and weapons. Live ammunition was fired within a few yards of us so that we had some idea as to what the real thing would be like.

I see from a letter which I had written to my father that on the morning of 17th February, we had endured a rough time. On one occasion, a few of us had to go over a part of the exercise again as the umpires did not think that we had become muddy enough!

By the afternoon our resistance had become fairly weak, but in spite of this there was to be an 'opposed landing'. And so we went over to a bay near Swanage and the name 'Chapman's Pool' will stay in some minds forever. The plan was that we should be rowed from one side of the bay and then out to sea a little way, before making a landing on the other side of the bay. As was customary on this course live ammunition was to be used by umpires and fired near to the boat when we were still at sea.

The boat was a sort of dinghy and the three Sections were to be rowed over in turn. In each section there were approximately twelve men. The actual rowing was to be done by the coast-guardsman who dipped his oars whilst we waited for the firing to start. As the firing started we were rowed off towards the shore. However it was soon noticed that water was coming into the boat. I think I was sitting amidships and as the water continued to come into the boat the supposed enemy continued to fire live ammunition, they did not appear to know of our predicament.

In no time the boat was filled with water, but we all behaved well, there was no panic. When the boat went under we were still about 30 yards from the shore, and weighed down with our equipment, clothing, backpack, army boots and steel helmets, not forgetting the rifles.

After all that had gone before that same day, our physical state was not very strong, and I had never been a strong swimmer anyway. I suppose the depth of the water was about 20 feet, so we were all out of our depth. My progress in the water was slow, and I went completely under twice. I did manage to float a little bit but it was a difficult situation. The bay was notorious as 'dangerous to swim.' The waters were fickle, shallows turned to large depths with quick effect. One of the instructors on the beach saw my difficulties and being a strong swimmer without equipment, he managed to reach me and helped me to shallower waters. Sadly, a Sergeant who had come with me from the Battalion was drowned. It was even more sad to realise that he had only been married for about a fortnight. He was the only one in our Section who didn't reach dry land. It hadn't helped that the tide was going out at the time. We lost a light machine gun and some rifles. When we arrived back at our billets I had a rub down and some whisky, and with the others I continued the course.

Eventually there were two Courts of Inquiry which I attended, one concerning our Sergeant and one over the loss of weapons. Apparently the bung had come out of the boat at that fatal time, but I think that the boat was overloaded and possibly unseaworthy. The boat of course might have been hit by the firing from the shore, or the rifle butts might have had an adverse effect on what happened. I suppose nowadays there would be more stringent enquiries, but this was wartime. On the Course was one of the Bentalls (Stores in Kingston etc.) and he was very keen to take the matter further, but I never heard any more about the unfortunate tragedy. Although I returned to the Battalion in what I thought was reasonable health, within 2 or 3 days I was feeling very feverish and I was quickly carted off to Shaftesbury Military Hospital.

I really did not know much about the first few days in hospital. I seemed to slip in and out of consciousness, and even when I was conscious it all seemed a nightmare. What I didn't know was that my family had received a telegram informing them that I was seriously ill with pneumonia. It seems I was on a danger list. I suppose that my experiences on the Course had resulted in delayed serious illness.

When my father received this news he made haste to go to Shaftesbury by train, and he stayed overnight in a Shaftesbury hotel. I vaguely remember his visit and his talks with the Ward Sister. I think that the latter was French Canadian, very efficient and kind. My father returned home and my mother and sister Edna and husband Colin came to visit and they stayed at the same hotel. I can remember Colin trying to get me to drink some tea, but apparently it was the May and Baker tablets (the name became known as penicillin) that were pumped into me that saved the day and managed to stop the downward trend.

I should say at this stage that there was one nurse who was looking after me in particular, and I subsequently learned that she had stayed by my bedside all night for some days. Then one day when I was feeling slightly more myself I heard some cheering. I asked the same nurse what all the fuss was about. She laughed and said that all the cheering was because I was at last taking in some food. I asked her what her name was and she said that her surname was Flower. "Flower," I repeated after her, "That's strange because there was a Flower on my OCTU course in Barmouth. In fact we went fishing together." She laughed: "That must have been my brother. It seems he was at the same OCTU as you." As she left the ward I could see that she was tall like her brother and had the same features.

Gradually I recovered and the day came when my family received a telegram telling them of my improvement. I was soon walking outside in the hospital grounds and gradually my strength came back. The air was still chilly, but to see the sun again with blue skies gave me hope for the future. As I left the hospital I gave my sincere thanks to the Staff and especially to the Ward Sister and 'Nurse Flower'.

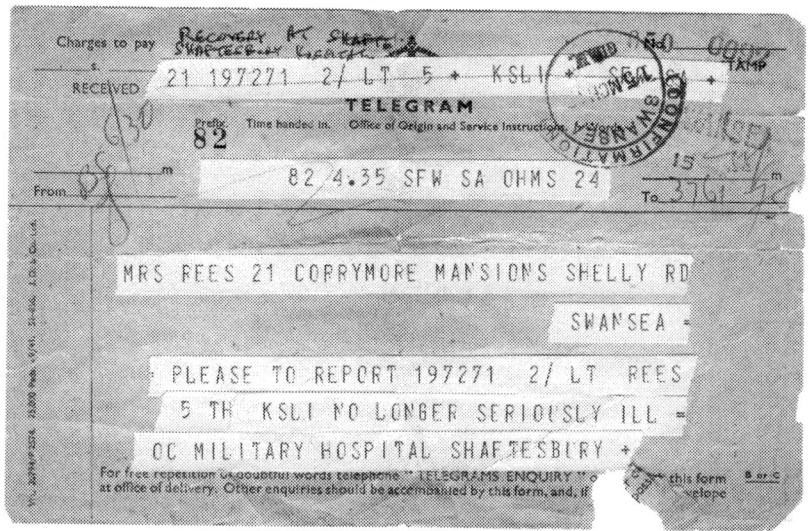

Telegram to my parents from Shaftesbury Military Hospital.

CHAPTER 7

Further Duties in Dorset, Involving a Plane Crash, Umpiring the Canadians and an Assignment at Divisional HQ

Whilst I was carrying out some duties on the Dorset coast in mid summer, I used to walk along the coastal path first thing in the morning. Although the invasion threat from Germany was no longer likely to materialise, the sea defences were still maintained at a high level. We had farm billets at West Bexington and there were routine patrols carried out on the seafront where there were gun emplacements. Almost immediately behind the seafront were areas of scaffolding, and some of these areas were mined. There was a pleasant pub at the top of the hill overlooking the sea.

I was walking along the coastal path early one morning. It was very misty but I could hear the drone of a plane which seemed to be in trouble. The mist prevented me from seeing where it was, but then it came out of the mist and crashed into the minefield which was protected by the scaffolding. The plane was one of ours but I could see that the two airmen had died in the crash. I felt helpless, but matters would have been better if we had been given proper maps of the minefields. A few days later two air officials came to the site and took sufficient information about the accident, and the bodies of the unfortunate airmen were removed from the awesome scene. The air officials seemed rather indifferent to it all, but then they had seen so much before along the same lines, and I've no doubt that they had become hardened to these tragedies. You just had to be that way. No doubt that the next of kin had already been informed.

Another exercise took place on this part of the coast near Lyme Regis, and as on a previous occasion I had been appointed as an umpire. The imagined exercise envisaged an opposed landing on the shore and the troops were Canadian. They seemed to be a pleasant lot, but their straggly slow progress after they had landed needed to be tightened up in every way. They were green in their ways but they would no doubt become an efficient organisation with more practice. A sign of their initiative was when someone pinched my motorbike from a lane near the beach. At least it showed initiative and they returned it to me in good condition after the exercise!

What I did not know at the time was that these Canadian troops were shortly to form part of the raiding force on Dieppe, and sadly they had many casualties. It should not have happened in my view, and junior officers like myself should have been allowed to give their verdict on such exercises. Dieppe was a gallant venture nevertheless.

In July 1942 the Battalion was in a tented camp on Bradford Down near Dorchester. However my platoon was sent to Divisional HQ to be the protective platoon providing security guards for a week. I was told that it was quite an honour for the platoon, and I slept in furnished quarters in a house with a proper bed. Luxury indeed!

Generally I had my meals in a Mess with other officers all of whom were of higher rank than me! There was one occasion when I had the honour of dining in the most senior Mess as a guest. The Divisional Commander was a Major General and so I was a guest of the General. This meant that I went into the dining room ahead of the General and I sat on his left side through dinner. The Major General's name was Butterworth. Anyway I was made to feel at ease, and he kindly asked me about my military career and where my home was. His ADC (a Lieutenant) was also very helpful.

I was really very proud of the smartness and support from my platoon, and there were no security problems to worry about. On one occasion I played cricket in a Divisional match, the first game I had played for a long time.

When I arrived back at Bradford Down near Dorchester there were plaudits for the platoon and I was told that it had been the best guard at Divisional HQ for some time.

Both Jack (Jackman) and I had now become full Lieutenants, so at least we were making some progress in that regard.

Then all of a sudden we were told that a draft of us were to be sent overseas, no dates being given. It only involved about six of us and apart from Jack and myself there were a few from the Herefordshires as well.

Matters in Russia at that time were very serious but we reckoned that our destination would probably be North Africa where the 8th Army, before too long, would be engaged with the enemy under Rommel.

CHAPTER 8

Transitory Experiences

Apart from Jack and myself, I can still remember a few of the names of the others on the draft. They included Johnny Walker, Hon Peter Grosvenor, Turp and a couple of others one of whom had medical experience. By and large they came from County infantry regiments just as we were. There were no Other Ranks attached to us. At first there was an air of excitement about it; all this was in late July 1942. However whether it was the lack of available shipping or the activities of U Boats or other factors, the weeks in transit became lengthened.

Certainly we had generous amounts of leave, but it was taxing for our families when we kept saying goodbye, not knowing if this would be our last visit or not.

July went by and then we did have a period in August when we were stationed at Osgodby Moor Camp near Market Rasen in Lincolnshire. Here we were attached to 8th Battalion Worcestershire Regiment. We were billeted in a separate Nissen hut and usually had our exercise by walking some miles into the small township of Market Rasen. The main meeting place for refreshment was a bakery/café here. It seemed that this enterprise was run by one family who had their own home attached thereto. All the family were very kind to us with their hospitality. Jack and I were even able to play some tennis here as the family had their own court. The local pub was also a welcome meeting house and there was a small cinema which was also well patronised. On the whole however, it was a quiet place and we always had to be within call at short notice.

We did manage to go to Lincoln occasionally and I did have the opportunity to visit Lincoln Cathedral. The size and quietude was awe inspiring amidst a war. Also Jack was able to arrange for his wife Joyce to visit Lincoln and stay at a comfortable hotel.

In early October we were transferred to 7th Battalion Royal West Kents, and we landed up at Dovercourt near Harwich. I think I had a short time with Peter Grosvenor in London and he was able to arrange for me to have a room at the Ritz for a night. The bedroom was of course very comfortable, but even at the Ritz it was powdered egg for breakfast.

I could sense that the time was now drawing near when we would leave the UK, and we were given an Army address to be used; RBK WW c/o Army Post Office 4000.

In Dovercourt we were billeted in a large house on the seafront. Dovercourt was quite pleasant being on the sea coast, and naval craft were always busying around. There was a large Wren building near and one evening we went to a hotel on the seafront for some beers. After some idle banter in the bar I strolled to the dance hall. A fair headed girl had just finished a dance but I was able to whirl her away to the tune of 'Three o'clock in the morning.' The dance ended shortly afterwards and

I noticed that Jack and the others had now gone back to the billets.

I escorted the young lady along the seafront at Dovercourt. Darkness now hid the destroyers lurking in the estuary. Apparently she was in the ATS but as she was on leave she was wearing civilian clothes.

We reached her home. "There's another dance next weekend, perhaps we'll meet again." She smiled pleasantly at me. "Yes," I said. I tried to respond with enthusiasm, but we had received orders that morning and I knew we would never meet again. Our Draft had a rendezvous in Glasgow on the following Sunday.

"Good luck," I waved to her and then made my way towards our billets. I ran up the stairs like a two year old, and barged open the door to the bedroom when, whoosh, a carefully laid trap of a bucket of water perched on the door, cascaded its contents over my battledress. There was a roar of laughter from the assembled throng. Water was everywhere so it seemed. I took it all with good grace but it was a hazard that lived with me for a long time.

It was a long train journey up to Scotland from Dovercourt and subsequently I regretted taking part in a game of blind brag to pass the time. By the time we neared the port of Glasgow I had lost nearly all my cash, and the only small comfort I could take was that there would be very little to spend one's money on anyway. We embarked on the troopship in darkness and we soon located our cabin which with the extra bunks accommodated most of us. The former passenger cruiser had been named 'Empress of Japan'; this name had been altered to 'Empress of Scotland'. Not surprising really! The eating venues or messes were reasonably comfortable and the food was generally good in all the circumstances, and drinks were available. There were some nursing staff aboard who mixed quite well with the men. I was agreeably surprised to find an old friend from Swansea on board; his name was Bobby Gibb and we had known each other since childhood. Jack and I and Bobby became involved in playing bridge some evenings, and it was good to enjoy some relaxation at that time.

There was usually lifeboat drill in the mornings, and we assembled at the designated place each time, with a typical bearded sailor was in charge of our draft. The weather was grey and rainy as we left the British Isles; after all it was October and winter was approaching fast. The convoy seemed quite large and it was comforting to see the destroyers and corvettes rushing about and shepherding us about, like a shepherd looking after his sheep.

There were already a few romances taking place on board, but it must have been well nigh impossible to have had private attractions.

We knew that the battle of Alamein had started and we could foresee that we were intended to catch up with them eventually and join the famous 8th Army. Time would tell.

Usually the troopships refuelled at Freetown but maybe the port was full of sea traffic or something, because we certainly didn't head for West Africa, we were steaming towards South America!

And that is what happened. After a long period on the high seas we arrived at San Salvador, and whilst refuelling was being attended to, we were able to look round the port a little. The local people seemed friendly but we wanted to be on our way again. It seemed strange that ship's lights were put on at night and I hoped that there were no U-Boats lurking in the neighbourhood!

A few days later we were on the high seas again and surrounded by our naval escorts as before. We were now heading for South Africa at last and the weather gradually hotted up. Progress seemed slow and one day we hardly moved at all whilst our naval ships busied about the area. About this time I managed to succumb to heat stroke, like some others. I retired to the sick bay as the unpleasant heat enwrapped my body. Gradually I recovered and felt better when on deck and revising our lifeboat drills once more.

Apparently we were heading for Durban, but the convoy had slowed down, it had been a long voyage. We had left home shores in October and a warm Christmas was anticipated in Durban. As we slowly made our way into the port we received a great welcome just like other convoys. A lady with a large megaphone stood on the quayside singing 'Land of Hope and Glory'; we cheered heartily and could scarcely believe that we had arrived.

The transit camp was already full up, and I was billeted in the City in a small hotel near the seafront. It was immediately impressive to see the spectacular buildings on the seafront, and with the weather so warm there were plenty of swimming pools we could take advantage of. Of course we all wondered how long we would be in Durban before we sailed for the last leg of the voyage, and meanwhile Christmas was approaching.

We took to Durban and the weather and the kindness of all the people living there. Apart from the rolling waves on the seafront and the swimming pools, there was a very impressive cinema; instead of the usual type of ceiling the motif of the ceiling was a dark blue sky with shining stars. It was very effective and gave the impression of really being in the open air. There were also pleasant places to go in the evening including dances and so on.

Before I left home my father had given me some addresses of former friends with whom he had done business, and also the phone number of his brother and family who lived in Johannesburg. I managed to phone them up and actually spoke to my Uncle Stanley. He and his wife kindly asked me to visit them over Christmas and at present I could see no reason for not doing so. I accepted accordingly.

It was quite common for a taxi driver to stop his vehicle and ask if he could transport you somewhere. It was certainly helpful in that heat!

Of course it couldn't last, and just as we were making our arrangements for the festive season we received orders to embark again. Sadly I had to phone my relatives to cancel my proposed break. I never did meet my uncle, whose voice sounded just like my father's.

This time we sailed on a large Dutch ship named the 'New Amsterdam.' There was only one destroyer escort but the liner cut through the waters at great speed. There was very little booze on the liner but as we had arrived at Christmas and the New Year, I remembered that I still had a bottle of Scotch in my kit. Of course the chaps on my draft had an inkling of this, so I did the decent thing! I shared it round and thus became a very popular person for a short while!

Eventually we reached the Suez Canal and Port Said, and then we moved on to the Middle East Infantry Depot in Egypt. In fact we landed on New Year's Eve and then there was a long road journey to the Depot.

It was somewhat ironic for me that soon after arriving at the Depot I was kept fit with another battle course, but it took place amidst the sand dunes, and was less of a challenge than the course in the UK.

I did bump into an acquaintance from the Queen's Westminsters named Trew, but life was a process of becoming acclimatised to the terrain. The days were warm but the nights were cold.

"Why don't we apply to join the Somaliland Camel Corps?" I thought that Jack was joking, but I think he had an acquaintance there. As the days ticked by that was what we did. The CO in charge of the camp sent for us, and he made it clear that the response to our proposal was negative. However, I felt that we had made our presence felt and that it might have a future value.

We did have a sort of get together one evening in a large tent, and apart from Jack and I, Hugh Brown and Bentall managed to turn up. The latter had been on that course with me in the UK. In fact we had to say goodbye to Bentall as he had been given compassionate leave for the UK. I think his father or some other relative was very ill at the time.

And then all of a sudden, after the long wait, I was being posted to the 1st Battalion Royal Sussex Regiment who were part of the 4th Indian Division in the British 8th Army. Unfortunately Jack and I had to part company; he was being posted to the Durham Light Infantry.

As my journey slowly headed westward, the period of transition was coming to an end. It was now late March. I started off on a train journey to El Adem, and then a plane journey to Castel

Benito near Tripoli, and finally a long and arduous road journey through the Mareth Line to join the 4th Indian Division in Tunisia.

I had reached the war zone.

CHAPTER 9

The Battles in North Africa.
Tunis – a Turning Point in History

I joined the 4th Indian Division just before a big attack was successfully launched. This attack was at Wadi Akirit and I was kept at Divisional Headquarters before the attack so that I could help with the searching of the prisoners of war and sending them back from our positions. They were mostly Italian but some were Germans. The Italians seemed only too glad to be sent to the prisoners' cage. The Germans seemed fed up and they disliked being mixed up with the Italians. We were heavily bombed at the time so it was not always safe even at Divisional Headquarters!

I then joined the Royal Sussex Regiment and I took over a platoon whose Commander had lost his life in the last battle. Major 'Bruno' Bryant was the Commander of our Company, C Company, and Bob Lumley another officer, was also in this Company. We were thus short of officers, but very experienced Sergeants took their place.

After a short period of time we moved forward again on a long road journey lasting three days. We were now in sight of the mountains which the Germans were holding. I felt it must surely be their last line of defence in Tunisia.

The Indian drivers delighted in making some of their dishes, but I still preferred the ordinary bully beef! There were masses of poppies growing in the countryside and wild flowers in abundance, and the fields were well cultivated by the local farmers. A psychological study of the British soldier; when he is really roughing it he doesn't grumble at all!

On April 22nd it was Good Friday, and previously on Palm Sunday we had moved into the forward line. At this time we were dive bombed, shelled and mortared. In addition we were covered in mosquito bites and there had been no food for 24 hours; we had thunder and lightening instead! I was struck quite forcefully by a large clod of earth thrown up by a mortar bomb.

On April 27th there was a temporary rest, but I was sent on a reconnaissance patrol in No Mans Land. It was the night of Easter Monday. We nearly bumped into a German patrol. Our job was to seek information and not to get into a fight if possible. We had to go to ground for some time. We had an Indian sapper with us, and he was the first to spot the German patrol. As we were being machine gunned from the hills we could make no further progress. The enemy were using powerful searchlights to sweep the area so we had to keep very low. Eventually we returned to our own lines without any casualties, but I would stress that when news reporters spoke of 'light patrol activity,' the activities were usually stressful and dangerous. Although we had been told that we might come across some mines we never did so.

I see from my notes that on Easter Sunday we had been at a church service amidst the fields of wildflowers with an accompaniment of heavy shelling in the distance. We were close enough to the enemy to see their flak going up towards our planes.

I can remember one position we were in which looked up at Djebel Garci. This seemed to be a steep craggy mountain which we understood was to be attacked by Indian troops. It was very unhealthy in our open positions on the plain. I shared a slit trench with a Corporal Bennett. He was a good soldier who told me how he had been in Cyprus, and how he hoped to revisit the island some time in the future.

Eventually I received orders to withdraw the platoon; the orders involved withdrawing through our own gun lines on a back bearing. This was an unpleasant course of action, as the nearer we trudged towards our own guns the more dangerous and noisy it seemed. Eventually we successfully accomplished this ordeal.

The 1st Army were apparently making some progress on the other front and we passed through Enfidaville at night. Enfidaville must have been a pleasant spot with picturesque cream coloured villas. Sadly it was now derelict and laid waste; a town deserted.

We had been given a number of mules for further mountain warfare. The mules didn't seem to mind the shelling, but the bombing seemed to worry them a little. A couple of them were killed in the last engagement.

By April 29th we had moved again prior to another big push towards a line of hills. In the olive groves we were sitting ducks for the enemy, and the general feeling was that it would be better to attack again rather than endure the accurate flak in our current trenches. 'Monty' issued another Order of the Day, and fighting on all fronts remained hard.

Sadly we lost Corporal Bennett at this stage in the shelling and mortaring at Enfidaville. It was quite upsetting; he would never see Cyprus again now.

Our 7th Indian Brigade had been selected to begin a big attack on the 8th Army Front, with Tebega Ridge as its objective. It was intended that the attack would be carried out at night but it was postponed. It was the key position now facing the 8th Army and was strongly defended.

Lt. Col. Firth who had been commanding the Battalion left to become a Brigadier, and his place had been taken by Lt. Col. Jack Glennie.

After the postponed attack it was eventually called off, and we were suddenly given orders to move at night to join the 1st Army. It was now the beginning of May and our Force from the 8th Army consisted of the 4th Indian Division, the 7th Armoured Division and the Guards Brigade. My platoon had to police the route at night time, quite an arduous job. We had to move west and north in our old desert sand coloured lorries. Dawn eventually came and we could now see and appreciate the countryside with the rolling hills, and the blazes of poppies and wildflowers. Eventually we met up with the 1st Army and it was strange to see their green camouflaged vehicles alongside our own transport. It was a heartening moment for all, and a historic meeting.

The main attack in the Medjez-El-Bab area with the two armies was completely successful, and then we had to take certain high features, so that the Gunner OPs (Observation Posts) could range on to the main road. The bridges were to be mined. The Bren Gun Carriers were in advance of our 'C' Company. The Carriers were commanded by Peter Cavalier. We all had to bear sustained mortaring and machine gunning. We dug in on the ridge as best we could and we lost another soldier. We were quite relieved when darkness came.

I should state at this time, that my batman who was with me, was named Len Mansfield. He was a seasoned soldier who had already seen a lot of action in France and the Western Desert. He was a great help to me at all times and our friendship has endured to this day. I still have the letter I wrote to my parents at this time in such words. He was already married with two children, and before the war he was a market gardener and horticulturist in Sussex.

During that historic night one of my Section Heads brought me a German Officer and two NCOs. They had come from the German lines waving a white flag. Apparently they wanted to surrender the whole of their battalion to us early the next morning. I informed Major Bryant of this, and early the next morning the sight was one for sore eyes, as they all started coming in to our lines. I was with Major Bryant and the Gunner Officer in our OP and we witnessed a great sight. Masses of German and Italian transport and personnel came streaming up the road, which had been cut. They all wished to surrender, and it certainly took some sorting out.

'C' Company then resumed their role of advanced guard with the Carriers who pushed on up the road. We followed the Carriers, and after passing a large amount of enemy equipment and transport, we suddenly stopped. Here a shell suddenly came out of the blue and I never did discover whether it was a German firing off his last shell or what. However, I did see Peter Cavalier with his Carriers guiding back a German Staff car which had a white flag on it. We proceeded up the road a little further and then we came across a sight I shall never forget. Masses of

Germans and Italians were lined up by their transport and they were having a roll call! After giving Heil Hitler salutes they were ready to be marched away! Meanwhile, General Von Armin (who had replaced Rommel) and his staff were located and they surrendered to our CO Jack Glennie.

I have to say that the Germans were still smart and surprisingly cheerful. They sang their German songs as they marched into captivity, and General Von Arnim's staff car was to be used by our CO. Quite recently in the Regimental Gazette its various travels were described. At one stage long after the war, I was kindly asked to meet a few old friends at the Regimental Museum in Eastbourne where the Staff Car was then located. Unfortunately I could not be there, but I was kindly sent a photograph of some of my friends of those times. They were photographed alongside the vehicle.

It was at St. Marie du Zit that General Von Arnim surrendered to our CO with the words, "I fought against the Iron Regiment during the last World War. Now I surrender myself to them in this World War."

When evening came all organised resistance ceased. Thousands of prisoners had been caged on Tunis Racecourse. It was now dark as light machine guns fired victory bursts of tracer shots into the night sky. I joined our CO in the caravan of General Von Arnim and we toasted the Allied victory with German brandy. However, it was a sobering thought that the German prisoners would possibly be sent by sea to Canada, whereas we would be thinking of battles ahead in Italy. As the reader will see later we reached Italy, land of rivers and mountains.

When I returned to my platoon, a single German plane came overhead and machine gunned us. The same plane then machine gunned a column of men marching on the road to Tunis. He must have thought they were Allied soldiers but in fact they were German prisoners; perhaps some of them never reached Canada.

At this stage I had happily settled in with the Royal Sussex, I became fully seconded to them. Also, I could honestly say in a letter home to my parents that the Indians were grand fighters.

Author just behind the line.

Peter Cavalier at head of Battalion in Bren Gun Carrier going to meet German Headquarter Staff.

Rounding-up German POW's.

Montgomery meeting King George VI in North Africa.

King George VI at Tripoli.

King George VI at Tripoli.

Harry Hawkes inspecting 'D' Company at Tripoli before the King's visit.

The Von-Armin Car. Held in the Royal Sussex Museum collection. From L to R: Major Bryant, Senior NCO, Colonel Buckeridge, Major R King, Senior NCO. The author was a platoon commander at the time of the capture of the armoured car.

Battalion Officers in Syria. The Battalion was moved to Syria for training after the end of the North African Campaign. Jack Glennie in plaster. Author top left.

CHAPTER 10

The Middle East Period
After the Tunisian Battles

Before leaving the battle zone I had to go through the motions of an infantry attack with my platoon in the fighting area. This was being photographed for some glossy magazine in the UK. In order to make it as realistic as possible we advanced over the area with bayonets fixed. Also a smoke screen was put down. The officer in charge of this exercise was Jack de Manio who we shall come across again later. Jack already had an MC but for this exercise he put down too much smoke. Whilst it was good to see his enthusiasm, the smoke, not unnaturally had a detrimental and stifling effect on the platoon. When we had recovered from this we repeated the exercise to satisfy the powers that be.

Before we started the main haul back to the Nile Delta in convoy, Major Bruno Bryant was given leave to the UK, and I had the responsibility of taking the Company back to Egypt.

Firstly we had a period of rest near Tripoli. The Battalion was reviewed here as King George VI had flown out to see the troops. You will see from the photographs the smartness of the seasoned soldiers, and in the photos can be seen Major Harry Hawkes in charge of his men.

Before we left Tripoli I went on a course for anti malarial control. I still have the notes for this course, and indeed the notes I made at the time for that fatal Battle Course in England.

And then our still battered and sandy coloured vehicles began to take us eastwards, and we moved as a Battalion. Sometimes the heat was intense and we were glad of the evening cool.

I remember that when we stopped at Benghazi for one of the rests we were a constant attraction for all the locusts around, and there were masses of locusts. They landed so softly on your body and skin that you did not know they were there. I decided that it might be better if I left my tent and went to a cinema that had been set up. I was starting to enjoy the humour of one of the Bing Crosby/Bob Hope films, the film included Dorothy Lamour of course, when all of a sudden the film stopped. My immediate reaction was that this was a technical hitch and that the film would restart shortly. How wrong I was. A message flashed up on the screen, I was to report to battalion Orders Group immediately. It was rather an anti climax when I was told that Jack Glennie wanted to give out fresh orders for the onward journey on the morrow.

Ah well!

We finally reached our destination at Dekheila near Alexandria, and here we remained for some time. The weather was quite hot during this period but we managed to do some training, and the sea was nearby. My stomach troubles returned at this time just as we had an intake of new officers who were senior to myself. I reverted to being a platoon commander again.

Leave was arranged as possible and I had some time off and went to Cairo. Prior to arriving at Cairo I had looked at the names and addresses my father had given to me. I had already written to a Mr. Constant who was manager of the Ottoman Bank in Cairo. I had previously opened an account with this bank, but of course on a Lieutenant's pay the amount in the account was not that great. Anyway, Mr. Constant was still manager of the bank and his office was impressive, with marble pillars and a high ceiling. As the cooling fans whirred overhead an Arab in his smart clothing brought in the local cash on a silver platter. The silver platter was no doubt worth more than the cash I had asked for!

However Mr. Constant had remembered my father and he was very kind. He invited me to his flat on the Nile with fine views, and he arranged visits for me to go with him to the Gezira Club. I believe that his son was engaged in the war elsewhere.

During the course of my stay in Cairo, I was walking down a crowded street one day when I felt someone brush against me. I checked my jacket. The thief, a young man, had stolen my pen. It was not of any great worth but it annoyed me considerably, and as I was pretty agile in those days I sprinted after him amidst the throng. Eventually I caught up with him and retrieved my pen!

Another canny trick of some of these thieves was at stations where kitbags had been loaded onto rolling stock which had grilles. If the base of the kitbag was near the air grilles they would use a knife to puncture the base of the kitbag and extract whatever was inside!

Unfortunately during the last days of my leave my stomach started playing up again. Mr. Constant had arranged for me to escort two WAAF ladies to the Mena House Hotel for dinner and to see the floodlit pyramids. Unfortunately I couldn't make it for health reasons. I had to apologise to him and I hoped the two ladies enjoyed the outing anyway.

Whilst we were at Dekheilia I had to serve as Defending Officer at a Court Martial. I did not know the soldiers involved as they were from another unit. You might remember that I had received some training in the UK on military law, but no doubt today, matters would have been handled differently.

Both cases involved desertion, and the question of intent was paramount.

I'm afraid at first I addressed the court sitting down. The President immediately ordered me to stand up in the Court when speaking! The first case was really an 'open and shut' case, and there were no grounds for getting a favourable result for the defendant. The second case however was borderline, and I considered that the question of intent had not been proven. The prisoner was given the lesser conviction of absence without leave and not one of desertion. I felt that I had done quite well, but even from the second defendant I did not get any sign of gratitude.

At this time I went on an Officers Patrol Course and then on a further Patrol Course for Officers and Men at the Divisional Patrol School near Haifa. I was on this course for a month, and in the meantime the Regiment had moved up to within a few miles of Bethlehem in Palestine as it was then known. This course was being run by Ben Clegg, a Royal Sussex officer with an MC. He was highly respected and experienced. The course was quite helpful but very exhausting. There was one occasion when I had to go on patrol by myself alone, and had to go for quite a time without food and live on the land. Pomegranates were my saving grace. In the evenings we lived a tented existence. I shared a tent with Wheeler and Fase. Wheeler had been in the Queen's

Westminsters but I hadn't come across him in those earlier days. Fase became Intelligence Officer, but sadly neither of them survived the later battles in Italy. We spent most evenings playing cards, there was nothing else to do. I usually lost at cards, as previously!

In Palestine I was able to visit Nazareth, the Sea of Galilee, Haifa, Acre Bethlehem, Jerusalem, Nablus and Tiberius. There was a large YMCA in Jerusalem for some good exercise, but I was unable to visit Jaffa and make contact with any of my father's friends, with whom in the old days he had arranged imports of oranges and grapefruit to the UK by ship.

After the Patrol Course I rejoined the Regiment who were still in Palestine, but on the advice of our Medical Officer Tim Reilly, I went into hospital in Jerusalem for observation and examination. I was in hospital for three weeks and had ten injections. I was assured that there were no ulcers in the stomach, but I thought that their diagnosis of indefinite dysentery did not fully explain matters.

This hospital had once been the Kaiser's palace, a strange but comfortable place for coping with illness. It so happened that I shared a small ward with our CO, Jack Glennie. The latter had his leg in plaster at that time where they were trying to rectify a problem. There had been no awkwardness over the sharing of quarters with Jack Glennie. He was always his natural self. He made me feel that although I was a subaltern we could still have an amicable relationship.

Meanwhile, the Regiment had moved to the other side of Tripoli in Syria and I rejoined them there. However, Tim Reilly soon realised that I was not completely fit so I had another few days in the Casualty Clearing Station.

We then had some more mountain warfare training, but I did manage to have a night in Beirut. Syria made a favourable impression on me and it seemed to be the most delightful part of the Middle East that I had visited.

A photograph taken at that time shows Jack Glennie with his leg in plaster. It was at this time that I learned that Jack de Manio had let himself down over fiddling with the Imprest Account. I daresay that he intended to rectify the situation if he could but regrettably he had to leave us and he was cashiered. He still retained his MC however. Much has been written about this event in Regimental journals etc., but I prefer to remember his bravery and geniality when he met up with old friends in reunions after the war. In peacetime of course he became a leading light with the BBC, both on the Today programmes and such programmes as those on Regimental bands.

After my night in Beirut I had hoped to visit the Cedars of Lebanon and Baalbeck but my planning was all in vain. Instead I found myself on a train very suddenly, as I was being sent on a months course to Abbassia near Cairo. Apparently the course was to be on Sherman tanks and I was to take some personnel with me. I was also told that after the course we would be going to the 'Brigade Reconnaissance Group' using Sherman tanks.

In the Army it was best to take some things with a pinch of salt, and I really could not believe that after all the infantry training this would happen. However, at the time other officers were quite envious that I would be in the Nile Delta for a while.

It turned out to be quite a strenuous month for me; it was all new work and it was anticipated that we were to go overseas again, fully re-equipped. The instructors on the course were very good and patient with us novices. I can still remember one of the instructors telling me that when I was controlling a Sherman tank, what the approximate cost of a new one would be! This undoubtedly brought mindful pressure on us to take care! There was an examination near the end of the course but the notes we had taken and the practical lessons gave us the foundations for the answers.

As a matter of interest there was a meeting at Teheran at that time between Roosevelt, Churchill and Stalin. It was that time of the war.

Anyway, by the time I had finished the course the main bulk of the Battalion had left for Italy, so I joined the rear party at Qassassin. It was here that I learnt that the Shermans were to be manned by Royal Armoured Corps personnel, and although I was given to understand that I might be involved with the Honey tanks manned by our 'Reconnaissance Group', the future looked as though I would be joining the Battalion again. No doubt by now my platoon would be commanded by someone else, and I felt sorrowful that I would be leaving the soldiers I had come to know so well. At least my batman, Len Mansfield, was still with me.

Our final encampment before leaving Egypt was near Alexandria, and at least for a time I was comfortably living in the Cecil Hotel. I usually had the dining room in the evening to myself, but one evening a table was joined by a Brigadier and one of the nurses who had been on out troopship some time ago. Clearly she had moved up in the world!

However, on New Years Eve I found myself somewhere on the sand out in the wilds, and I only had one bottle of beer. There was no Mess. Did I see the New Year in? No I didn't! 1944 here we come!

Of course we had missed the invasion of Sicily, but my friend Jack from earlier days had not. He had been with the Durham Light Infantry in Sicily and had been badly wounded in a night attack. At dawn he had found himself in a German position near Catania. Apparently he had been wounded in the arm, the hand and the small of the back. He found himself unable to walk. At first light a few Germans crawled to where he was, put a bandage on him and then cleared off because of our troop movements.

Apparently he was in that spot for a long time and the Germans would not give him any water; in fact they even stole his water bottle. There was heavy fighting around the Primasola Bridge. Eventually he managed to crawl to the road and he was picked up by an enemy tracked vehicle. Then he was taken to their Regimental Aid Post (RAP) and later taken to Catania Hospital. An operation was carried out here and then he was sent on to Messina. From here the enemy had intended to transfer him to Italy by hospital ship. However the hospital ships were so full of their own wounded that poor old Jack was left behind. Eventually the Americans arrived and he was evacuated to North Africa. Thus he ended up in an American hospital. It was to be a long time before he was anything like fit again.

When the Sicily operations had been completed the main body of our Battalion were shipped to Southern Italy, and by January 1944, I was on the Rear party heading across the Mediterranean to join them and enter Europe at last!

CHAPTER 11

Back in Europe – Southern Italy

At last I was on my way back to Europe and crossing the Mediterranean towards Southern Italy. It was January 1944, and although it was now winter none of us on the Rear party expected that the Mediterranean would be so rough and uninviting. Plates and cutlery slithered across the tables and the smallish vessel was not built for such a sea passage.

At least I suppose the weather kept the enemy at bay and eventually we landed at Taranto in the south. The weather here was raw and blustery. From Taranto we went by train to Potenza and then there was a road journey to join our Brigade moving north through Foggia to Lanciano.

It was very cold after the Middle East and there was plenty of mud, mud, mud. One loses all sense of time and some nights we slept out in the open, which did not cheer us up in that weather! The countryside seemed poverty stricken, and I'm sure that some of my readers will have experienced such weather in the south at that time of the year. Certainly when we were there the local people lacked food and clothes, and generally lived in sordid squalor. On the whole however, the Italians seemed generally pleased to see us and to be freed from the German yoke. The scenery at least was very impressive.

Eventually I caught up with the Battalion at Lanciano and it was an uplifting experience to see old friends again, and the CO Jack Glennie. He was still uncertain as to whether I was to join the Brigade Reconnaissance Group or not, and when the Battalion went into the line I had the task of looking after all the transport behind the River Sangro.

It was a strange war here; the civilians did not take much notice of the shelling and it was not difficult to spot the villages which the Germans were holding.

Lanciano was shelled during the night and we sustained casualties. At one stage I took cover in a villa where a lady member of the household was playing the piano whilst the shells kept coming over. Surreal really, but why not?

For the task of looking after the transport I was stationed in one of the humble peasant's cottages. They were very kind and we kept warm by the open fire. They also gave us welcome wine and eggs, but certainly this was a part of Italy that Mussolini had not been able to bring up to an acceptable living standard.

At the beginning of February I was posted to the Bren Gun Carrier Platoon in a new Company formed, known as 'Support Company.' It made sense for me to take over the Carriers when I recalled that I once had a similar position in Dorset in England.

The weather began to dry up and I was stationed at Castel-frentano nearby to Lanciano for a while. Fortunately the Germans hardly ever shelled this village.

CHAPTER 12

The Battles at Cassino

'Cassino was the nearest thing to Passchendale which the Second War had to offer.' The Sunday Times, 13th January 1974.

We were only at Castelfrentano for a short time. Suddenly the Division had orders to move around to the American 5th Army front from the 8th Army front. (Shades of North Africa!)

I anticipated that there must be something brewing for the 4th Indian Division again, and for the move I had to take the Carrier Platoon by train using 'Flats' for the tracked vehicles from a local station. When we arrived at the station nothing seemed to be happening. Eventually a pyjama clad RTO (Railway Transport Officer) appeared. I found his garb somewhat irritating since we had been up on the move from an early hour, and since when had we last seen pyjamas! In blunt terms I complained about the absence of our train and I stressed the importance of swift action. Just before my patience gave out a train with the flats arrived. The Carrier Platoon then had to load the carriers onto the flats and chain them down. So eventually we moved slowly northwards towards our destination. I remember that we passed Caserta where the 5th Army Headquarters were stationed at that time.

Gradually as the weak sun came out the train seemed to gather speed and the lads struck up a song – 'Finiculi Finicula'. It seemed an appropriate vocal for the countryside through which we were passing; rivers and mountains. Had they known what the near future involved, I doubt whether their cheerfulness would have been so outgoing.

Meanwhile I should state that the American 5th Army had been attacking over the Rapido River towards the Liri Valley, whilst a French Force was beginning to attack through the mountains in the north towards the Gustav Line.

However the German inner defensive system consisted of steep mountains including Monte Cairo (5000 feet high), Monte Cassino and Monastery Hill with the Monastery.

Clearly the enemy had impressive views of any moves made by the Allies. They had well camouflaged positions for their weaponry with mortars in support. The town of Cassino itself was also strongly defended with self propelled guns and gun emplacements amongst the rocky mountainous terrain. To make life even more difficult there were mines and wire, artillery and Nebelwerfers (mortars firing several mortar bombs one after the other). It was obviously going to be a tough nut to crack, particularly at this time of year, but the Anzio bridgehead had to be relieved as soon as possible.

After cutting across the Rapido Valley, Highway 6 then cut across the Liri Valley. The mountainous range had a series of ridges with hollows and small crests; there were large boulders and rocky outcrops. I remember that before we moved forward to replace some Americans, we were corralled in some muddy ditches and hollows in the ground. The battalion had already endured long marches, and I could not envisage the Carriers being of much help in these mountains.

In fact when the Battalion trekked up the mountains to relieve the Americans, the Carriers had to be left behind, but the personnel including myself took up positions on the lower slopes of mount Cairo and Mount Castellone to render support as necessary to the rifle companies. The same situation applied to the Anti-Tank Platoon. The Battalion, when in the line, could only be reached by mules, and supplies had to be taken up every night by mules under the control of the Carrier platoon personnel.

The rifle companies relieved the Americans way up in the mountains very near to Cassino, and they were overlooking Monastery Hill with the famous Monastery. The desolate feature where the Americans had striven and where some of their dead lay, was known as Point 593. Those numbers were never forgotten by those who fought there at one time or another.

Thus, the Carrier Platoon personnel were to help with the servicing and supply to the rifle companies. Being based on the lower slopes of Mount Cairo and Mount Castellone, there was constant shelling on these positions, and then under cover of darkness the personnel had to get the food supplies up the mountains every night.

Then one night, Joe Upton, the Second in Command of the Battalion, told me to take a special delivery of ammunition and other arms to the forward Battalion Headquarters. This was wanted quickly as the Battalion was going to make an attack with all the rifle companies. 'C' Company had gone forward the night before, but they had been forced to retire. They had made good progress, but they had been handicapped by a lack of grenades and other arms. Eventually I arrived at Tactical Headquarters on the night of the Battalion attack with the mule train which had been shelled on the way up the mountains. The loads had arrived in time. Jack Glennie asked me to wait at Tactical Headquarters until the attack was over in case there was anything else they required.

The Regimental Aid Post was also established in the stone enclosure. I was never to forget that night. It has to be remembered that Point 593 was the most forward salient, and it dominated all the other major features. In early February 1944, the near side of point 593 was held by the Americans and the other slope was held by the Germans. This meant that elements of the elite German 1st Parachute Division were approximately 60 yards away from the Royal Sussex soldiers.

The history of the 4th Indian Division states that on the morning of the relief from the Americans by the 7th Indian Brigade, the following was the position,

'When dawn broke 4/16ths Punjabis looked across the intervening falling ground into the rear walls of the Monastery, almost within touching distance, as one of the officers put it. Every window peered into the Indian lines. The Royal Sussex were even more uncomfortably situated. Immediately in front of their foxholes and shallow sangars (built up stone emplacements) loomed the rocky crest of Point 593, with the ruins of a small fort on its summit. The slopes were shaggy with great boulders and the infantry must make its way alone.'

After the Company attack there was now to be a Battallion attack, and yet again the casualties were heavy, both of officers and men . The terrain and defences of Point 593 were a tough nut to crack. The CO had asked me to stay at battalion Headquarters during the attack in case there were other requirements over supplies to be brought up.

It wasn't long before the first casualties were borne into the stone hovel and many good men were lost that night. It was ghastly to see the wounded coming into the shelter as the MO and the Padre did their best to save lives. One officer, Captain Gains lost his life, and already 11 officers had been evacuated as wounded. The Battalion had to come back to their original positions. Although the attack by the Gurkhas on Monastery Hill was nearly successful they too had to retire.

The attacks really had needed more preparation and planning. It should be said that General Tuker who commanded the Division had been forced to go to Naples to obtain a book on the details of the Monastery, such as the thickness of the walls and so on. All these matters had been pointed out to Higher Command, but there was insistency on urgency in order to draw off German troops from the Anzio Bridgehead. There were many brave deeds that night, for example, Lt. Dennis Cox with Tommy gun and grenades, destroyed two spandau posts. Then he crawled forward and destroyed an enemy sangar, but he became badly wounded. Later on he was awarded a DSO. There were also sheer drops in the terrain which added to the difficulties.

Three of the Company Commanders were Major Ben Dalton, Harry Hawkes and John Gratton, and they all acquitted themselves so well. Alas, Tiger Brand was no longer alive.

The Companies had been much depleted, and I've no doubt that the Germans had suffered heavy casualties as well.

The Gurkhas had attacked Monastery Hill and were nearly successful, but they too had to retire.

There were many 'ifs' about the situation and in an ideal world the attacks would have had more preparation, especially in the abominable weather conditions. All these points were made by our CO and Brigadier to higher-ups, but the priority was to draw off German troops from the Anzio Bridgehead.

It was with a heavy heart filled with sadness that I made my way in the darkness back to Rear Headquarters. As I anticipated however, I did not stay there more than 48 hours. Jack Glennie sent for myself, John Wilson and Tony Jones (all specialist officers) to help make up the shortages in the Rifle Companies.

So Len Mansfield and I started to go up to Point 593 again; how eerie it was to see the Monastery again, you immediately felt that the eyes were on one from the half smashed windows. When we arrived at Point 593, the CO remembered that we were once in 'C' Company, so we were posted to this Company which was commanded by Ben Dalton. He and the others had already had a gruelling time of it. The Battalion had been formed into 3 Companies, and No. 13 Platoon, my old Platoon had been washed out. So I took over No.15 Platoon, the Company now consisting of No's. 14 and 15 Platoons, and one Platoon from 'D' Company which sadly had been split up.

Our Company was in a stone enclave at the summit of Point 593, and Len Mansfield and I used part of an existing trench and reinforced it with heavy stonework. Then night came down to blanket our activities. The night seemed awash with shelling, mortaring and machine gun fire like a night wake up call. As I sheltered in our sangar I wondered what was in store for us now. We were in the most forward salient on the front.

It was not unnatural that casualties were still accruing; the ominous call for stretcher bearers was always with us. A fine, experienced and brave officer Laurie Weeks, and Ken Wheeler who had been in the Queen's Westminsters like myself, both lost their lives within a few days; Ken Wheeler had been on Patrol Courses with me. It was a sad and grim time indeed, but it was stressed to us how very important it was for us to hold our positions, especially now that fresh troops were to attack across the plain to Cassino town and Monastery Hill.

The two American Divisions, the 34th and 36th Divisions had become virtually non existent. The American 5th Army under General Mark Clark had suffered severe losses, and there were more heavy losses on the Anzio Bridgehead. Whereas originally the Anzio Bridgehead had been planned to relieve the main forces pushing northwards, matters had now become reversed. Now the main forces were being asked to relieve the Anzio Bridgehead.

The next thing that happened was the bombing of the Monastery Hill feature, in which very much damage was done to the Monastery itself and the town of Cassino below. For anyone attacking the town of Cassino itself, it meant that even more boulders were strewn around, making it very difficult for tanks to make progress. Further Indian Battalions were going to attack Monastery Hill from the lower slopes away from us, with the New Zealanders attacking the town. However a stalemate was reached. On Point 593 we received bombs from our airplanes, and shelling from our own guns, we were so far forward.

As a Company we then held a different part of the feature, and we were now face on to the Monastery. It was maintained that Monastery Hill had to be destroyed and this meant that the Monastery came under attack as well. It was always my belief that the Germans at least, had observation posts in the Monastery and from our new positions we used to take shots at the Germans in daylight hours. I found that the best weapon we had for this was a Browning light machine gun which the Americans appeared to have left behind. The Germans were usually by the front walls.

The aerial attack on the Monastery Hill began on the morning of February 15th at 0930 hours. The roar of high level bombers was heard in the sky. The Flying Fortresses dropped their blockbusters; the ground shook all around. Twelve bombs fell in our Brigade area. There were also casualties from pieces of masonry from the Monastery cascading through the air. Then the medium bombers struck more accurately. It was the first occasion on which bombers from the UK attacked a target in Italy, then continued on to North Africa to re-arm for another attack en route for home.

It was very sad to see how the Monastery had suffered. It was re built some years ago. Given the fact that Monastery Hill had to be taken out as a stronghold, I do not see how the Monastery itself could escape considerable damage.

At the time my new sangar had one vertical sheer cliff wall and the surrounds were built up with stones and rocks around. The improvised roofing was not effective, and it rained constantly at very cold temperatures.

Unfortunately it was about this time that Len Mansfield had to be evacuated with his condition of severe rheumatism and lumbago. We all missed his presence. Around 11pm each night the mules would arrive with a hot meal and liquids including a rum ration. They also brought up mail from home, eagerly awaited.

My nights were interrupted as far as sleep was concerned. Enemy shells, mortars and tracer bullets fired on fixed lines kept me awake a lot, and then there were the Very lights. Also, Jack Glennie had not forgotten my patrol experience, and I had to carry out several reconnaissance patrols. This meant taking a few of the quietest men out with me into No Man's Land. As we were so near the enemy I tended to go round through the lines of another Company first. Which was alright if you knew the password! One of our Corporals who was Irish seemed to enjoy the challenge and was always making sure that I was all right. Usually I had to patrol as near to Albanetta House as I could get. I couldn't take anyone who was going to make a noise or had a cough. On the other hand I had to detail individuals as fairly as possible.

Certainly we ascertained that Albanetta House was occupied, as well as the ruins of it and the surrounding area. We could hear the usual noises of occupation and what sounded like water being distributed. Eventually we made our way slowly back to our own lines. When we returned we were challenged by the Company whose lines we had traversed, so we had to whisper the password again.

Whilst I was away the Platoon was being commanded by Sergeant Hammett. He was very reliable in all ways. There was always a stand-to at dawn and dusk, and I shared the night watch with Sergeant Hammett when I was not out on patrol.

There was one evening just before dark when activity was very pronounced, that a member of the platoon had stood up in his sangar and received a bullet straight to his head. Although he had not actually been seen by the enemy, it was sheer misfortune that he died. Later on, when Sergeant Hammett and I went over the man's personal effects, he had kept everything so neatly in his small pack, everything that he needed to be there. It was all surprisingly clean. He had been a regular soldier. "A good man Sir," said Sgt. Hammett. "Yes, yes I know," I sighed as I left the Section Post, but such a loss made me angry.

One morning when it wasn't actually raining, the Padre arrived at my sangar. I wasn't expecting him and I thought he was being too bold. "I'm just paying a visit", he managed to speak first. "Do you realise that it is St. David's Day, 1st March?" "No you lose all sense of time and day here," I paused, "But thank you for coming anyway." I knew what a strain the battles must have had on him with all the burial services and help he had given to the wounded; he felt such losses deeply I knew. He rose to go and shook my hand. Before he left he remarked, "D H Lawrence once stayed in the Monastery and wrote a description of it later on in his life." I could have replied that his description would bear no relation to what I could write, but the Padre was already on his way back to Battalion Advanced Headquarters.

There was one reconnaissance patrol that we carried out to try and pin point enemy positions on the near ridges and to give an account of the general terrain, with especial reference to mines and booby traps. Before we left the visibility was very poor and I suggested that the patrol was delayed for 24 hours, but apparently no postponement could be made. Extra care would be needed if that was possible, and in the very misty weather it would be difficult to spot trip wires that let off flares. Machine guns would no doubt have been trained on the trip wires. As usual we had a getaway man if the worst happened. Otherwise we kept close together; a Very light suddenly shot up but that time we were able to lie flat before the scene was lit up. A fit of coughing in the cold damp air could have been fatal. We crawled forward on our bellies; now and again we would stop and listen to see if we could locate enemy positions. Then suddenly we heard the ominous sound of pick and shovel a short distance away to our front. There was a surge of relief as we could now report back on the terrain and on enemy positions. Eventually we returned to our own positions, the mist still heavy and damp. Keeping direction was difficult even with a compass. Someone stumbled on a boulder and a very light shot up again. Bullets were now ricocheting on the stones and some whined overhead. The enemy obviously suspected our presence and the machine gun fire was dangerously close. We were making headway towards our own lines but it was slow progress. Then there was a Wumph! Wumph! We dived in a hole, then we were about to start off again when there was another Wumph! We were temporarily unable to move further. It was one of those dreadful mortars, nebelwerfers, when the mortar bombs come over one after another. As we had stirred things up I decided it was best to push on back to our lines fairly quickly. We reached the forward outposts of 'A' Company, and I was soon giving my report. "Well done," I muttered to my companions, "Go and get some rest now, if Jerry will let you."

At this time I should emphasise what a tremendous job was done by the stretcher bearers and the signallers, the latter were constantly having to go into dangerous territory to mend the broken lines and so on.

The news of a relief soon travels round a Battalion, but our first relief was of a partial nature only. It was on March 5th that the 2nd Camerons of 11th Brigade of our Division relieved us on Point 593. We then took up a counter attack role in a curious enclave 500 yards to the rear, known as 'The Bowl.'

The relief was not carried out easily at such close proximity to the enemy. It had to be done at night and at the same time as the German positions were constantly shelled and mortared. It must have been one of the wettest nights going, and the platoons literally slithered their way down to the Bowl. It was a pitch black night and as we picked our way down the boulder strewn path several of the platoon fell over from time to time. It was the furthest we had exercised our legs for many a day. We were guided to a piece of sloping ground in the Bowl, and then improvised a shelter for the night. We tried to erect some overhead cover with groundsheets and gas capes, as the icy rain poured down in torrents. We were now soaked through and I was glad to see the dawn. At first light I could see that we were on one side of three hillsides, which formed the flat bottomed enclave. A few hours later we were moved to a different hillside.

Here we had a fine view looking over the plains and upwards towards a shell scarred area known as the Snakes Head because of its shape. Once platoon positions were allotted we were able to dig trenches and erect overhead bivouac cover, suitably camouflaged.

The first tasks in the Bowl were concerned with maintenance. To be able to stand up in the open and clean one's body and weapons, was a great morale booster, and for once the sun came out and the sky was a clear blue. Even in Italy the spring must come sometime, even if not yet. I visited the other platoon and Company Headquarters where Major Dalton was in a good humour. He had become impressed with Sergeant Hammett and was in a mind to get him promoted as and when he could.

This limited amount of exercise meant that appetites were gradually restored, and we began to look forward to the daily arrival of the muleteers with the rations. It was good to see Sergeant Kemsley of the Carrier platoon again when he came up with the mules. Now and again the cooks managed to send up a few doughnuts which were very popular.

I spent many hours with Sergeant Hammett at this time and before dusk descended we would sit and chat outside my sangar. He was a married man with a child and he often spoke to me of his wife and home in Ilfracombe. Amongst other things he was full of praise for the expertise of his wife in the culinary arts, and it was a matter of conjecture as to which dish he preferred the most. "I could do with some eggs and chips right now," he said. I bade him to cease as my mouth watered thinking of my mother's home cooking.

"Do you think we could use the 38 set to get Vera Lynn on the Forces programme Sir?" he asked. "No don't do that," I replied. "We have to conserve the juice in the bloody thing". "It's our turn to take a patrol to Snakes Head tomorrow evening Sir". "OK," I said, "We'll sort out that one in the morning."

A day or so later, Ben Dalton sent for me and said that an opportunity had arisen for someone to go to an Officers' Mobile Shop at Rear Battalion Headquarters, and bring up some fresh shirts and other necessities for the Officers. He asked me if I would like to make the trip, and within a few hours I was on my way down the mule track, accompanied by the Doc who was going to make a visit to the ADMS (Assistant Director of Medical Services).

It had been such an age since I had last seen this track, littered on each side with the debris of war, the shell and mortar holes being an unhealthy reminder that it did not pay to delay too long on the way. It was good to see the Doc looking so cheerful after his casualty point on Point 593 had taken such a pasting from the shelling and mortaring. An advanced dressing station had been set up to the rear of Point 593, and the casualties were then hand carried a distance of nearly 4 miles to Ambulance Jeep Head. Here a forward dressing station operated, and this station had the misfortune to lose 16 stretcher bearers from a single shell. 400 stretcher bearers and ambulance drivers were always 'on the go' up and down the steep, treacherous track. Within the Division, during this period between battles, casualties continued at a rate of nearly 100 each day. The main dressing station was at St. Michele; this consisted of surgical units and a blood transfusion team, but even this station received shelling, one officer losing an arm whilst attending a patient.

"Well my boy, it's been quite a gruelling time," the Doc remarked. He could always be relied on to refer to one as 'my boy.'

"Yes, and we are not out of the wood yet by a long way" I added.

"Never mind my boy. See that you get a good feed down in the valley today, and have a rest."

We passed a number of Indian porters on the way, and also the teams of stretcher bearers in their slit trenches about 400 yards apart, waiting for the daily toll of casualties. As we arrived at Cairo village, the low lying cumulus gave way to a sky of cobalt. Here we were given a jeep with a driver, and driven along the route known as the 'Mad Mile' to Rear Headquarters.

We had lunch with Quartermaster Blackmore, Blackie as we called him, and it did not take me long to get together the shirts and necessities which I had come to collect. The Doc also carried out his mission expeditiously and it was not long before we were on our way back. The few hours away from mortar shelling had been a pleasant respite however.

As dusk came down over the hills I reported back to Major Dalton who informed me that the German propaganda machine was active. The leaflets they had dropped had an amusing aspect often enough, as those in Urdu often arrived in the Royal Sussex area, whereas those in English often descended on the 4/16th Punjabis or the 1/2 Gurkhas.

A few reinforcements arrived and we continued our standing patrols on Snakes Head Ridge during the hours of darkness. We took up static positions there, and it was a most unhealthy position to be in from the constant mortaring. One had to be very alert as the German paratroopers were often probing in this area.

It was now March 14th and another assault on Cassino began with the signal, 'Bradman will be batting tomorrow'. Operation Dickens it was called. A big attack was launched on Cassino by the New Zealanders and bombers dropped 1100 tons of bombs on the target area. It is believed that a battalion of the German 3rd parachute Regiment all died in the ruins of Cassino town. Some of the bombers went astray, and Army Headquarters at Venafro about 20 miles away received hits. Our Divisional 'B' Echelon also received some bombing, and 50 men and 100 mules were hit.

The vast rubble heaps in Cassino town meant that the New Zealand tanks could not make progress to try and mop up. Castle Hill, the first objective was taken, but bitter fighting ensued with the fanatical paratroopers, who were concealed behind ledges and boulders. A Company of 1/9 Gurkhas had miraculously infiltrated onto Hangman's Hill near the Monastery walls and were reinforced. Supplies were dropped to these valiant Gurkhas by plane. It was now the plan for the 1/4 Essex and 1/9 Gurkhas to strike for the Monastery itself from Hangman's Hill.

However, that night the Germans launched a heavy Battalion attack against Castle Hill. The German paratroopers were pinned down, but they reorganised and launched a second attack under cover of a smoke screen. The attack again broke down, but a third assault was launched. This assault was also beaten off, but the situation was serious. A Company of the 2/7th Gurkhas reached the Castle, and in spite of 75 survivors of the Essex reaching the Gurkhas on Hangman's Hill, the attack on the Monastery was called off in view of the heavy battles that had been fought.

I have mentioned the battles of the 5th Indian Brigade at this time as it explains why it was considered that a diversionary scheme by our brigade to the rear of the Monastery might be helpful. The forces of our Brigade to take part in this operation consisted of our Brigade Reconnaissance Squadron, together with 19 Sherman tanks, 21 light tanks from an American Tank Battalion and from a New Zealand Armoured Regiment and 'C' Company of our Battalion; that was us! I understood from Major Ben Dalton that our Company was only being deployed in a minor role, and would not be committed in the attack unless it would be advantageous and necessary.

24 hours before the skirmish was due to take place, I joined the other officers of the Company in a reconnaissance of the tank harbour area, which was known as Madras Circus. This area in the Upper Rapido Valley was flanked by the French positions, and we walked up to their positions on the side of a hill. Here we were given a hospitable reception including a glass of wine, a

very pleasant surprise! Full liaison was established, and we were able to view part of the tank track that had been built up from the rear, a notable engineering feat by the Indian Sappers, for the terrain was steep and offered no natural tank routes.

This tank area was not far from our Company positions in the Bowl, and at first light the following morning C Company joined our tank friends in Madras Circus. It had been decided to leave our new officers behind in the Bowl for the time being. At 0600 hours the tanks moved off, and the wireless messages at first were very encouraging. They had penetrated past the Massa Albeneta, and they had been involved in successful shoots on enemy outposts on the western slopes of Point 479 and 593.

The Commander of the column decided to push on towards the rear of the Monastery, and the swiftness of the operation caught the enemy by surprise. In fact, intercepted wireless messages revealed that the local German Commander advised the German High Command that an infantry attack must be expected. In retrospect, perhaps, the opinion could be formed that if this tank attack had been supported by a large number of infantry, the Monastery defences would have crumbled, but alas, one Company of infantry could at best have achieved very little even if committed.

It so happened that the Corps Commander had reached a decision that if the tanks obtained positions from which the Monastery could effectively be fired on, the force on Hangman's Hill was to strike for the crest. The tanks went on to encircle the main enemy defences, but then encountered a narrow defile with steep slopes. This defile was mined and under heavy mortar and machine gun fire. The leading tank 'brewed up' and blocked the track. The Shermans could not progress, the going was too steep.

They withdrew, and the light tanks tried to force their way up to the rear walls of the Monastery.

As the day wore on we received reports of tank casualties, and after 12 tanks had been knocked out, the remaining tanks were ordered to withdraw under cover of darkness. Meanwhile, during the hours of daylight the enemy had been searching out the tank harbour area where we were. There was heavy shelling, and I was caught out in the open at an observation post during a bad spell of this. God! I thought, I must be hit this time if they keep up the shelling. The sinister whirr of shrapnel was all around, and one of our platoons had serious casualties including direct hits on slit trenches. I saw two men dive into their slit trench, leaving their haversacks just outside the slit trench. When the shelling stopped they were dead, but the haversacks were intact.

In general, the infantry were always pleased to have tanks with them during an attack, but we were very exposed when the enemy were trying to cause maximum damage and havoc in the tank assembly area. This was our worrying position. I made my way from the observation post to the platoon area. Platoon Headquarters was established along a low ditch which afforded a certain amount of natural cover, but we had dug in, nevertheless. My slit trench was sited next to that of Sergeant Hammett.

As darkness fell Major Ben Dalton told me that the Company was withdrawing to our positions In the Bowl, but our Platoon was to remain here. We were instructed to take out a patrol to one of the abandoned derelict tanks, where certain documents had to be retrieved. In order to verify the actual tank concerned we were to have guides from the Brigade Reconnaissance

Squadron with us, and I was only to take a few selected personnel from the Platoon. One of my main worries was that our French allies on the flank were very close to the route I was to take. Their forward machine gun posts were very active. I had my patrol ready long before the guides arrived. When they did eventually arrive I asked them somewhat angrily, "Do you know where this bloody tank is?"

"Yes Sir," they answered in unison.

"Well I hope it's not far off. I've no wish to make a courtesy call on the Monastery tonight."

We set out in single file, the guides keeping to the fore with me. We advanced along the valley between the hills. Visibility was good I thought. One of the patrol started coughing badly. Thinking of our French friends as well as the enemy, I halted the patrol. I found out who the culprit was and sent him back to our lines.

On we went, covering the ground remarkably quickly. The first derelict tank loomed up ahead, one track completely off. It was not our objective though. I slowed down our progress somewhat. God knows what we might run up against. Another tank which was burnt out was silhouetted on the right, an eerie monster.

I was able to follow the tank tracks now and then there was a nudge from one of the guides as we approached the object of our mission. The tank had well and truly taken a pounding and whilst the members of my patrol formed a defensive ring round the tank, the two guides searched the tank itself. They did not find the documents, so I looked myself without success.

"They're not there damn it!" I muttered inwardly. Great risks for so little, someone should be blamed I thought. I gave orders for the guns to be spiked (neutralised), and we carried out this task on two or three tanks in the area. Therefore the patrol was not in vain, but I felt more than a little angry.

And so we made the return journey to the Platoon area, the frustration being shared by us all. The remaining tanks were still harbouring in and around our positions. Sergeant Hammett had been on duty ever since I had been out on patrol, and he came over to my slit trench. He asked if he could take a rest. I said that I would take over now, but just as I was getting out of my hole in the ground the earth shook with a sudden avalanche of shelling right in the Platoon area. This shelling is coming from the flank I thought, they're searching out those tanks, and then I thought it was all up. A heavy shell....I prayed, perhaps it's only concussion.... the earth, it's coming down on top of you. You fool, fight your way out," I cried inwardly. I crawled out of what remained of the caved in slit trench. One of my mortar team came up, "Sergeant Hammett is dead Sir."

"No he can't be", I said to myself. "I was talking to him a minute ago."

A minute; so much can happen in so short a time. He wasn't even on duty at the time, I thought. Of all the tricks of Fate, this was a grim blow to me. My own trench was now useless, and as a further pasting of the area opened up, I dived behind a tank. Ping! The shrapnel hit the tanks and tracks, pieces flying in all directions.

"Is the Platoon Commander here?" A voice queried in the darkness, the voice of our Company runner.

"Yes, what is it?"

"The Company Commander says that you are to rejoin the Company in the Bowl."

Just as well I thought, otherwise we will all be wiped out here. The Platoon quickly assembled, and we ascended the hillside leading to the Bowl.

As the German Nebelwerfers carried out their nightly mortaring, I broke the tragic news to Major Dalton of the death of Sergeant Hammett.

"And the documents in the tank. Did you give them to the tank people?"

"They weren't even there," I answered.

"Good God! I'll see that someone hears about this. By the way, I have some news. The 6th Royal West Kents from 78th Division have relieved the 1st and 4th Battalion the Essex Regiment in the Castle area, and have been subjected to serious enemy attack."

"How did it go?"

"The attack was beaten off, and they've taken about 40 prisoners."

"That's better. Think I'll try and get some shut eye now."

I crawled into my trench in the Bowl, feeling a great sense of loss. One of the new replacement officers called out to me; "Hello there. How did it go?" It was Tom Manners.

"So so. I'll tell you about it some day. Goodnight."

Dear God. Why did you have to do it? He had so much to live for.

As the early mist cleared in the morning, the first thing I noticed was that whilst we had been away supporting the tanks, our positions in the Bowl had been bombed from the air by German planes; some of the bivouacs had been torn to shreds. At least we had missed all that and showed that ill luck did not dog our steps at every twist and turn.

After an early breakfast I gave orders for maintenance on our weapons to be carried out. For a while all was peaceful on the hillside. However just before noon the Bosche struck at us with mortars; the mortaring didn't stop all day. Clearly the enemy now realised that we were making good use of the Bowl. It was not long before the first casualties were reported.

During the day, five of my Platoon were evacuated as wounded, and after the death the previous day of Sergeant Hammett, this was a great blow to me. It must be remembered that all ranks had endured a gruelling time in the past weeks, and after all the attacks and positional changes on Point 593, it was dire luck to be wounded at this stage of the operations.

Corporal Osgood had now become Platoon Sergeant, and he was a very solid type, thoroughly reliable, and remained unperturbed during all these experiences. I would like to say that throughout the whole operation I was always well supported by the NCOs in the Platoon, and they assisted me in organising the evacuation of the wounded; we could lose no time with the long carry by the stretcher bearers to the rear.

As dusk came the mortaring eased off, but I stressed that no unnecessary movement was to be made. After the mule train had delivered our food I felt very tired after all that had gone before in the last 48 hours. Sleep was easy to come by.

During the next few days rumour went round that we were soon to relieve the Camerons on Point 593! The rumours were soon confirmed, and at the same time we were told that a general relief would soon be accomplished. That word, "Relief," how quickly it could pass from mouth to mouth in the world of the infantryman, and we all knew that the 78th Battle Axe Division was in the area.

If the weather does not deteriorate there is a reasonable chance of a relief soon, I thought.

The battles had now reached a stalemate, both sides being in a weak state. When I broke the news to the Platoon that we were to relieve the Camerons on Point 593, they took it in good heart, feeling I am sure that things were almost as bad here in the Bowl as they were elsewhere. The Jocks also deserved a rest, if the positions in the Bowl could still be called a rest area. The advantage in the Bowl was that there were times when you could stand up and stretch your legs without being sniped at. But you still had to watch out for mortars.

I remembered the treacherous night when we had made the descent from Point 593 to the Bowl, and I decided that whilst it was still daylight I would refresh my memory of the route we were to take that night for the ascent. I set off unaccompanied over the shoulder of the Bowl and made my way across the rough terrain to the Advanced Dressing Station. From here I climbed towards the saddle and reached Kesselring's former dugout, which I had passed in the earlier days. Cautiously I crawled to a vantage point above the dug out, and I trained the binoculars first on Point 593, and then on the Monastery.

As though the eyes were attracted to this vista of destruction, I gazed with awe at the devastation all around. For once there was an aura of quietude, not a living soul in sight, but my binoculars picked out the human dead, the animal dead and the vegetation dead. This was a terrible sight for the 20th century. I've seen more than enough I thought. I would now get back quickly to the Bowl; there was too much exposure here. At least it seemed to me on the way back that my limbs were stronger than when we were here before. Back down to the Bowl where we read the last mail from home.

Soon it was time to prepare the kit for the evening trek up to Point 593. We seemed to live from hour to hour, I thought. Major Dalton summoned us for final orders, although there was no more information about a general relief. The night grew cold, and soon the plains below were swathed in darkness. Would I ever see those plains again? The civilised world seemed so far away; to us all the word 'Naples' meant civilisation. A day in Naples, the biggest place yet liberated in Europe. 'Naples,' the password to life again; 'see Naples and die' was all wrong; to see Naples again would mean to live.

"Platoon ready to move off Sir," Sergeant Osman interrupted my thoughts. "Right, we'll move up the track in single file. It's not wet and slippery like last time. Let's hope that our guns and mortars keep the Monastery occupied during the relief." The depleted Platoon moved off across the Bowl to begin the ascent once again to Point 593, and as we started to climb I could hear the German mortars striking at the area of the Snakes Head as if to say, 'we know you're on your way.'

We arrived back to our old positions on Point 593 without mishap, and not unnaturally the Camerons were pleased to see us. The relief had been carried out very speedily, and by arrangement the Monastery was heavily shelled and mortared during the takeover. We had not had any casualties, and the Camerons bade us farewell. My old sangar which I had previously occupied in this Platoon position was no longer useable, it just wasn't there! So I shared an existing sangar with Sergeant Osgood. Now he was broad in the beam and as we also had to accommodate our equipment and the field telephone, the reader can imagine that there was little room to move!

Anyway, I visited the Section posts and impressed on the Section Commanders the necessity of lying low during the hours of daylight. Apparently the Bosche snipers had become even more active now.

There was even more tinned food lying about now and it was almost impossible to move about without making a clatter with one's boots. It meant of course, that the ration columns had been very faithful to their tasks, but appetites in this position were pitifully weak.

Dawn came and the usual 'stand to'. It was a bad policy to share the same sangar with the Platoon Sergeant. One direct hit and we're both dead. How long would it take for the main relief to arrive, I wondered?

Everything seemed very quiet, and the morning passed peacefully enough. Just as I was beginning to doze off at midday, the telephone lines from Battalion headquarters to Company Headquarters somehow became crossed, and unwittingly I overheard a conversation between Jack Glennie and Ben Dalton.

"Brigade headquarters are anxious to have positive information that Jerry is still on Point 593, there's a theory that he may have pulled back off the hill. I suggest that Roy Rees be warned for a patrol." Jack Glennie waited for a reply.

"He has already done three patrols since the operations began," replied Ben.

"There is no one else available; however it may not be necessary." The CO put the phone down at the same time as I did. There was no more to be said. It will be just my luck to catch a packet before the main relief, I thought. A daylight patrol from our part of Point 593 to the enemy part would have been more difficult; to me it pointed to 'no return'.

I reported the fault on the telephone lines to Ben Dalton, and I visualised once again the signallers sallying forth to put the lines in order. I must stress again, the dangerous work done by the signallers. With the air filled with shrapnel, they had to find the break or faults in the line, and then repair the damage. They were exposed to all the hazards and yet they carried out their vital work.

My phone rang. "Sunray here." It was Ben Dalton.

"Yes Sir."

"There was talk of carrying out a patrol, but the information has been obtained from another source now. The Bosche are still on Point 593."

"You're telling me!" I responded, as some rifle grenades landed in our area. I put the phone down, but I did appreciate the way that our Company Commander really looked after the Company as best he could.

Meanwhile Sergeant Osgood had disappeared. Where the hell has he gone, I thought. He should have waited until dusk before wandering off. Presently he returned with tins of milk, there was an abundance of them in the area.

"What are you doing?" I asked.

"The lads will enjoy a drink on the way down," he replied.

"I suppose that you were the cause of those grenades," I grunted. "Still thinking of the relief, eh?"

"I suppose it will come one day." There was a query in his voice.

"You should never answer a question by asking another, but I suppose you're right, it will come one day," I said; but as I made this remark I noticed that flakes of snow were descending on us. We looked at each other meaningfully, and not before long the positions were blanketed with Arctic whiteness. Good God! Have we not had enough of all the elements? Surely, I thought, as March nears its end we can turn our backs on winter, if not on Point 593.

I began to think that the snow might well alter the plans for the relief, but then I had a message from Ben Dalton to say that a representative from the Northampton's' Advance party would be with me after dark. At long last....can it be that the Division is pulling out? I lay down and thought of all we'd gone through, and thanked God that I was still alive.

I should at this stage make mention of the fact that on March 23rd the Corps offensive was abandoned, and the forces on Hangman's Hill had to be withdrawn. This was an isolated garrison where there had been a heavy toll of casualties. They had been supplied daily with air droppings. Amongst the items which had failed to reach the garrison were radio batteries, and communications were very much upset. It was therefore deemed unwise to risk wireless communication for the withdrawal plans.

Three Officer volunteers were selected for the task of reaching Hangman's Hill, so that they could deliver orders by word of mouth. The three officers selected were an Englishman, a Scot and a Welshman, and each officer set out on the night of March 24th/25th with a carrier pigeon. The carrier pigeons were appropriately named St. George, St. Andrew and St. David. Two of the officers reached Hangman's Hill but the third was forced to return to Castle Hill. A system of signals was arranged, and a difficult withdrawal was carried out from these positions.

And so it was that on the night of March 25th/26th the 5th Battalion of the Northamptonshire Regiment climbed the hills to Point 593 to relieve the depleted ranks of our Brigade. The difficult and complicated relief was carried out in a fierce blizzard, and as the Northamptons moved into our positions under cover of darkness, a barrage from our guns and mortars kept the enemy positions quiet on Point 593 and the Monastery.

I realised that our journey was to be a long one and would prove a great strain on weakened limbs and muscles. We moved down the snow covered track on the first stage of our journey to the Bowl; the Platoon was heavily laden with equipment and, in addition, we carried down to the bowl, fatal casualties for burial. The going was heavy, and the steep slopes were very slippery. Jerry mortars started to whine overhead. I hope that they are not mortaring the track was my first thought at that time. It was difficult to keep the Platoon together when they were so heavily laden, and at regular intervals we stopped for the stragglers to catch up.

At last we arrived at the Bowl, and I checked to see that all the Platoon were present. The Bowl presented an unusual sight and there seemed to be a steady stream of sub units reporting to check points before proceeding on their downward journey.

The remainder of our Company had already left the Bowl, and after a few minutes rest I started the further stages of the descent. The going was still hard, and our legs were soon to become naggingly weak. Once again we went past the First Aid Posts and mortar positions, down, down, down the mule track, and Cairo village loomed up in the blackness of night. The base of the hills at last!

It was at this stage that Corporal Osgood produced the tins of milk, they proved very welcome to our parched throats. We carried on with our trudging gait as we drank the cool liquid, never stopping in our trail. We knew that we had to meet the transport on the far side of the open valley before daylight.

As usual there was unceasing activity in the Advanced Dressing Station in the ruins of Cairo village, and stretcher cases were being taken to the motor ambulance car head. At last we reached the road to the rear, it was the first time that aching limbs and weak bodies had set foot on a road for six weeks. Even here we realised that Jerry was liable to shell the whole area, and although extremely exhausted we trudged on determinedly past 'Windy Corner' and eventually the 'Mad Mile', so frequently shelled. This time we traversed the area without mishap. Yet even now, as a following storm rolled up in the sky the Monastery stood out, towering over the landscape and dominating in its darkened silhouette. Every minute or so I noticed someone or other in the Platoon involuntarily look over his shoulder to peer up at the Monastery. No doubt there was a feeling that up in the mountains in their sangars they were on level terms, but here on the road in the valley it was night alone that hid us from the enemy eyes in and around the ruins.

The mule trains passed us on their way up towards the relieving Division, and I thought back to our first night when we in our turn had crossed that valley of indecision into the hills of death. May the fates be kind to the relieving forces, and may they have better weather.

As dawn came we reached the transport on the other side of the valley, and in their true spirit of comradeship those who were left of the platoon after the recent actions, weakly helped one another up to the tailboard of the lorry. We were at last ready to move off.

I took one last look at the Monastery, standing out bloody but unbowed, but with an air of serene quiet in this early light; the snow still cast a white blanket over all.

The dawn still found many men of other units out in the open valley, but the blizzard protected them as they moved carefully in their weak state to the rendezvous with the transport.

As our own transport moved off towards Venafro, I lit a cigarette and felt an inward peace I had not known for so long. We left our lorry near Venafro and I found our Company site in a pleasant olive grove. It all seemed very strange and peaceful after nearly two months of the noise of guns and other weapons of war.

I was even able to have a hot shower, a change of clothing and a camp bed again. What supreme luxury!

Len Mansfield my batman was back with me as it happened although he was not really fit. I could see that he was glad to be back with the Platoon.

The sun shone through the trees in the early morning, and I struggled with the razor to shave off my bearded growth. A welcome breakfast and then that booster, the arrival of mail. Avidly I read the news from home and after reading the final air letter my eyes involuntarily closed. I was lying on a bed again, and I was soon in the arms of Morpheus. I awoke some time later and Ben Dalton told me that the CO wanted to see me. There was a comforting smile on his face. I made my way to Jack Glennie's tent. He looked understandably tired, but he said some kind words to me as he promoted me to a Captain. So it wasn't long before Len Mansfield added the extra pip to my shoulder on the epaulette.

During these operations, more than 4000 men of the Division were killed or wounded, and the men felt that they had earned a rest.

I suppose that I was fortunate to have a spot of leave with a few others, and we visited Naples firstly, war scarred Naples where it was a pleasant relief to see civilisation again, with the shops, vino bars, the clubs and the pretty women, the reunion with old friends and a toast to absent ones.

Even more, the leave to Ravello on the lovely Sorrento peninsular was so restful, with its magnificent views of the landscape. Our hotel was set amidst the lemon groves, so beautifully terraced, and the quiet was so relaxing. Within this peninsular the King and Queen of Italy were living in a state of exile in their own country.

I thought of all the friends from the Battalion who were now lost, they would never see Italy when it was peaceful and beautiful, more than that they would never see England again. I sipped my wine and wondered what lay ahead. The road would be rough I was sure, but with all the Allies we would win through in the end.

One fine spring day I heard the ominous sound of a motor bike climbing the zigzag route to our haven. As it came nearer I realised that time here was up and we would shortly be back with the Battalion. I looked down on the quiet lane below, two small Italian boys were kicking a football around, learning to expostulate and throw their arms about in an Italianate manner. How long would it be before they could get back to a normal life as they grew up, I wondered.

We had held on at Cassino and it wasn't long with the better weather, better preparation and stronger forces before the Anzio Bridgehead was relieved; the enemy losses were heavy. On May 16th the Monastery positions were attacked by the Polish Corps after the 8th Indian Division and the 4th British Division had pierced the Gustav Line along the Liri River. The Poles attacked through Point 593, and after fierce fighting, the enemy was finally driven from these heights. Over 100 Poles lost their lives. There was desperate fighting west of the Monastery, but the Allies finally conquered.

After the war and some years later on, it was possible to travel by bus from Cassino to the Monastery in 20 minutes, and the battle scars gradually were diminished. The town with its new buildings became a popular stopping place for tourists going from Naples to Rome. The Abbey was rebuilt and the trees on the hillsides began to grow again. On the fertile plain dominated by Monte Cassino there is a Commonwealth Memorial in a Garden of Remembrance. Roundabout, the locals once again cultivate their small areas of land with corn or vines, and around the cemeteries the borders shine with gazanias and other flowers. In early summer you will see varieties of butterflies and with the azure sky you may even wonder if the bloodiest of battles ever took place here. But the cemeteries bear witness to the many men of 15 nations who died here. The breakthrough to Rome had been made, and the Allies invaded France from England. The restful aftermath was limited as we shall see.

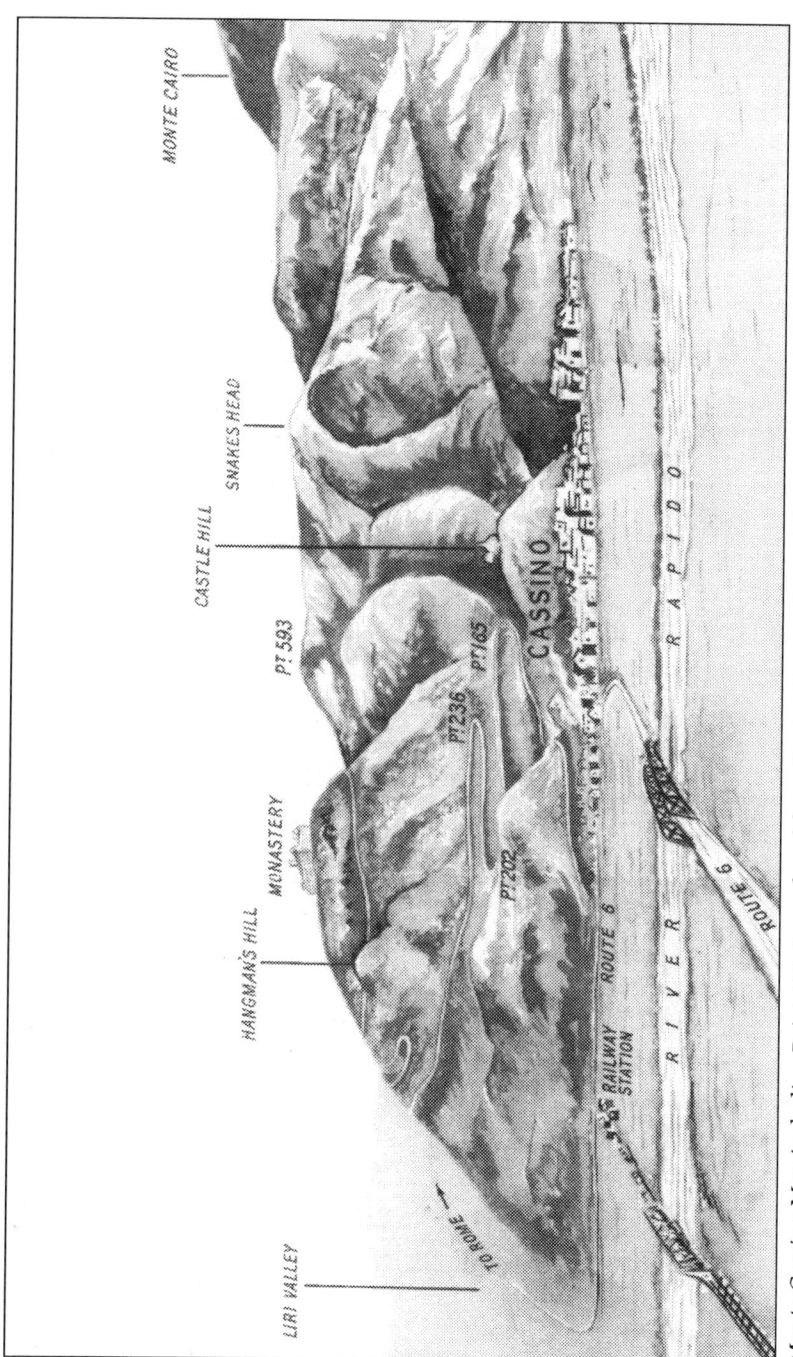

Monte Cassino Map including Point 593. Reproduced from *Cassino Portrait of a Battle* by Fred Majdalany.

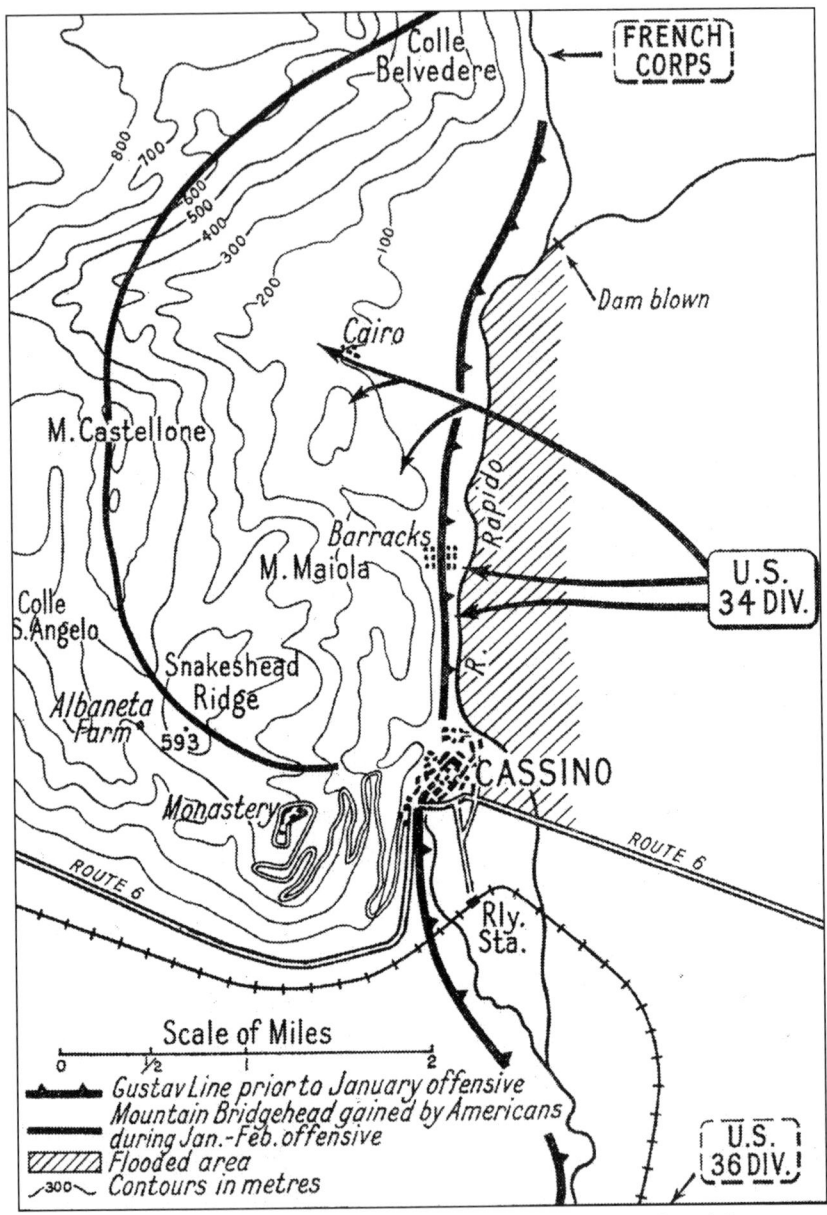

Upper Rapido Bridgehead. Showing Snakeshead Ridge. Reproduced from *Cassino Portrait of a Battle* by Fred Majdalany.

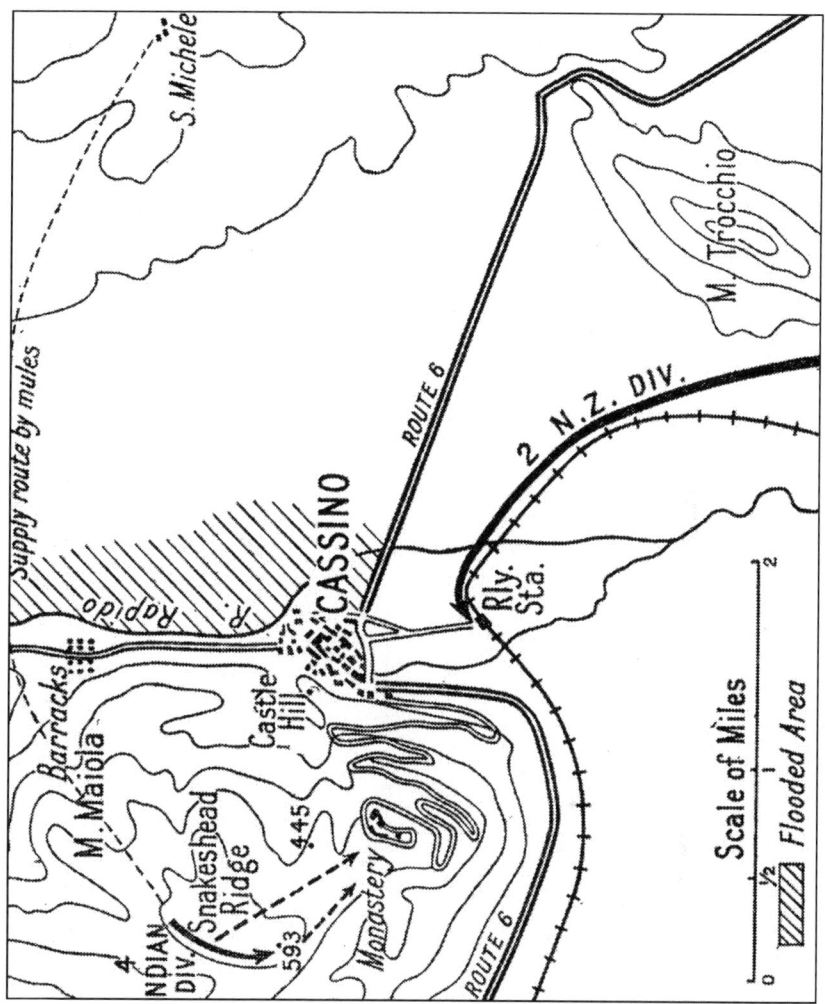

Map of Second Battle showing Cassino Town. Reproduced from *Cassino Portrait of a Battle* by Fred Majdalany.

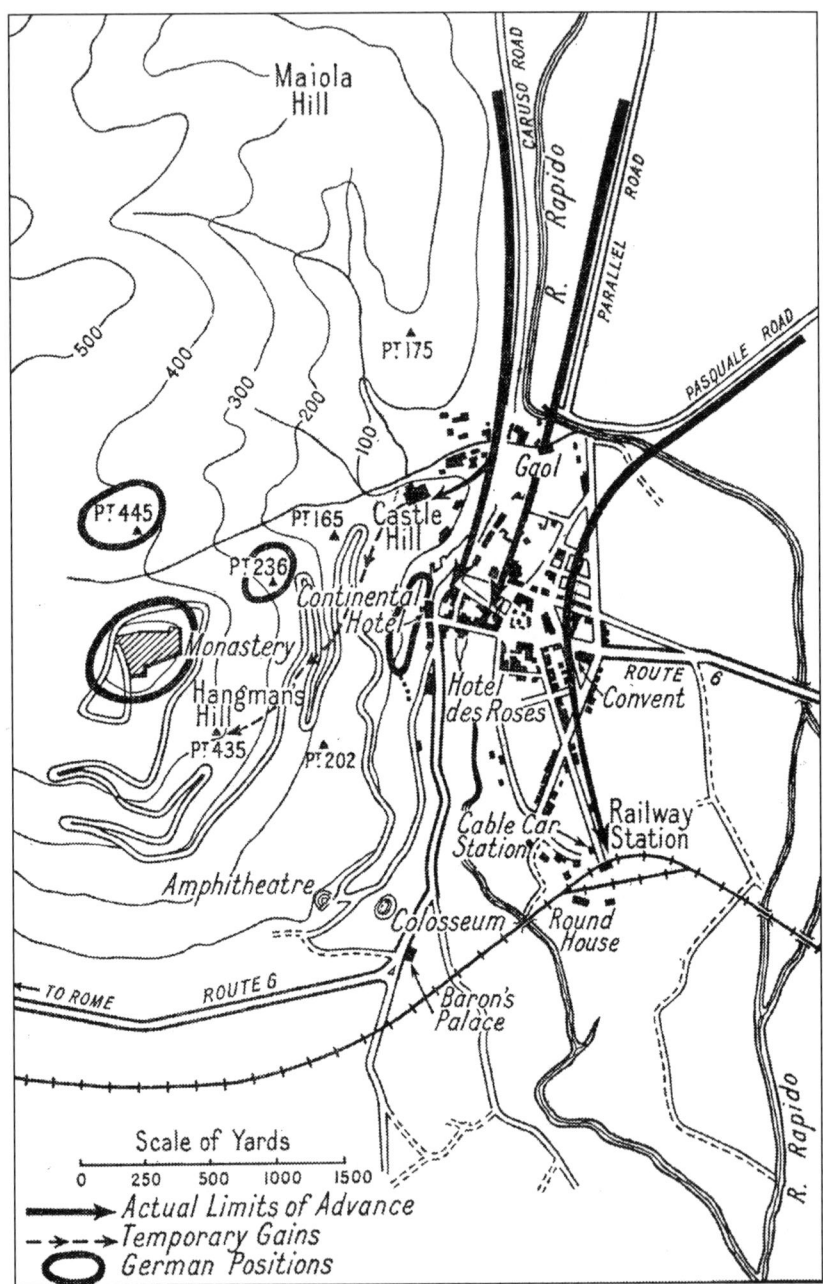

Map of Third Battle of Cassino. Reproduced from *Cassino Portrait of a Battle* by Fred Majdalany.

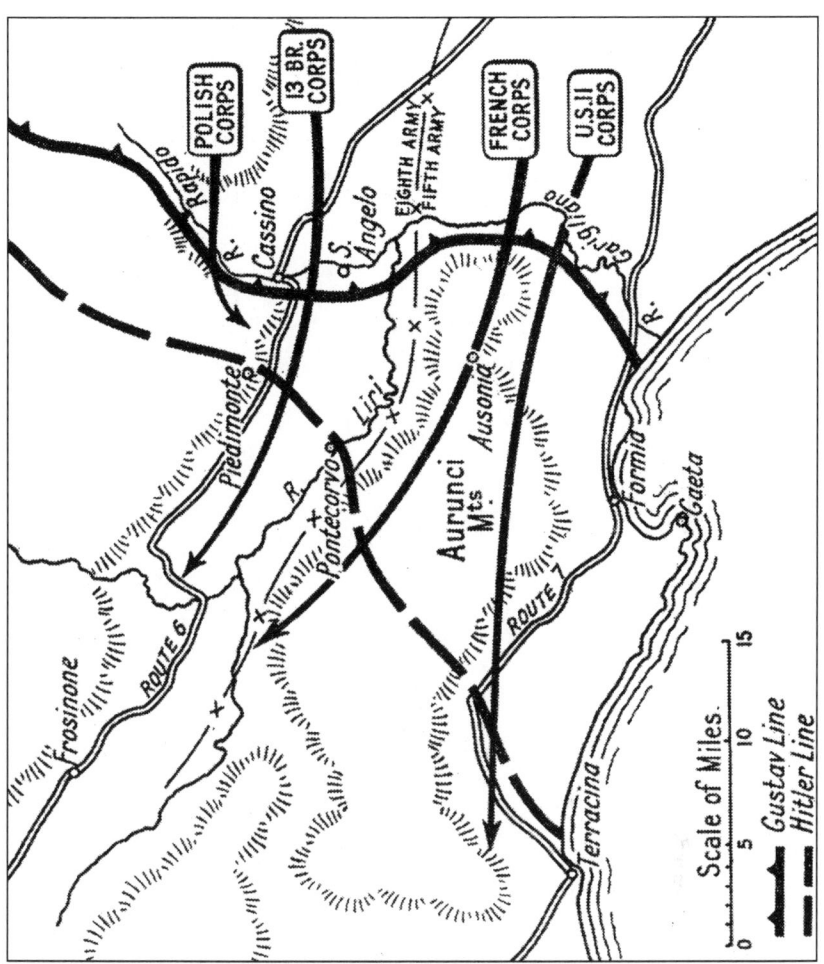

Map of Fourth Battle of Cassino showing larger forces for the successful Spring Offensive including the Polish Corps. Reproduced from *Cassino Portrait of a Battle* by Fred Majdalany.

The Monastery itself. Reproduced from *Cassino Portrait of a Battle* by Fred Majdalany.

Monastery Courtyard and Cloister before air bombardment. Reproduced from *Cassino Portrait of a Battle* by Fred Majdalany.

Monastery Courtyard and Cloister after the air bombardment. Reproduced from *Cassino Portrait of a Battle* by Fred Majdalany.

Point 593 where The Royal Sussex Regiment were so heavily engaged. Reproduced from *Cassino Portrait of a Battle* by Fred Majdalany.

Chapter 13

The Adriatic Front. 8th Army Again

We moved back to the 8th Army once more and I was given some leave at a pleasant rest camp near Bari. This time I was not recalled from leave! I see that my notes say that I was able to get to Bari fairly easily. Apart from seeing one or two films and a couple of shows, I was able to see some opera and a symphony concert. Bari itself was quite a pleasant place. One of the shows included the personal appearance of Marlene Dietrich. Unfortunately she had a bad cold and throat at the time, so when she came on stage she apologised for not being able to sing. She went on to say "What would the boys like me to do?" The immediate response from the soldier audience was a loud series of wolf whistles! I am glad to say that Len Mansfield had some leave as well at the time.

When I was back at the battalion there had been hospital admissions amongst the officers, and I took over a different Platoon in 'C' Company. This meant that I had now commanded every Platoon in the Company.

We had a fairly peaceful time in this part of the line near Orsognia, which was helpful in the circumstances after our very severe times with the 5th Army.

However, we then moved to a Sector near Arielli where it was not quite so peaceful. I did another three patrols here, and I was living in a trench, the nearest house was very tumbledown and filthy. The weather was now very good and the malaria season started. We were now clothed in khaki drill although at night I used my battledress as a defence against the mosquitoes.

The main offensive at Cassino had now started and reports indicated that we had cracked the Gustav Line this time. Where we were at present we did have a few casualties with people walking on mines and booby traps, and we did receive some shelling and mortaring landing very close.

As we were reserve Company there were many patrols to be undertaken, particularly as identifications of the enemy were required. Altogether I did six patrols, two of them being fighting patrols. For the last of these fighting patrols I had to carry out a daylight patrol just after 'D' Company did a Company raid before us. They were on our right. I felt that it was a little strange that after all the patrolling at night I had done through the left hand positions, I was now about to do a daylight raid across our front. Anyway, a large amount of shelling and mortaring was put down beforehand after which we made rapid progress towards the enemy lines. The ruined enemy posts seemed empty at first but then we did capture two prisoners in our quest. We would have taken a third prisoner but as he tried to escape he had to be shot. We learnt that 'D' Company also took four prisoners. Lt. Col. G.A. Phelps who had taken over from Jack Glennie was no doubt pleased with the results and visited the Platoon. I was dozing at the time so he did not disturb me but he praised the Platoon.

Shortly after this Army photographers took photographs of our Platoon and 'D' Company under Harry Hawkes. I was given a few days leave in Naples but on one's own I can't say that I had a great time. It was no doubt an innovation to be billeted in a building that was the temporary home of an ENSA troop who did their best to entertain the soldiery on the stage. They were Scottish and all female and regarded me with some suspicion! After all they did not know me and were slightly concerned with the male intrusion!

Charactature of author drawn in Naples during the liberation of the city.

One evening I sought out the Officers Club and the bar within. There was a large number of officers present as one would expect, but glancing over the throng I could not see anyone I knew. Not surprising really. Several of them seemed to be going through the vino list, a very unwise thing to do! I had a drink or two and then left. The next morning I was on my way back to the battalion. Some Italian Regiments then relieved us, they were now Allies remember, and we relieved the 10th Indian Division in the Ortona Sector. Suddenly I had Orders to leave the battalion temporarily and go on a three week tactical course at the Central Mediterranean Training Centre at Benevento. The course was a pleasant change and very interesting. Being in the 4th Indian Division they realised that I had a sound knowledge of the subjects and I was able to give useful advice on the tactical exercises.

Meanwhile, the Second Front had started, and here in Italy our Armies had taken Rome. As my notes say the news was very encouraging.

Back with the battalion and then we were engaged in mountain warfare training near Campobasso. Whilst I had been away I learnt with regret that we had lost another officer, Stanley Fase by name. There had also been many changes in the Battalion. Ben Dalton, Harry Hawkes and John Gratton had all gone to Staff College, Doc Tim Reilly had gone to Divisional headquarters, and two others had gone to Brigade Headquarters. One other officer had gone away for an operation on his eyes, and Len Mansfield had been badly burnt by a cooker and was in hospital.

I should mention that when we were in the positions from which we launched our raids to capture prisoners, there was one tragic occurrence. The soldiers had been warned not to vacate their positions unless absolutely necessary as there were scattered mines about. Unfortunately one of my Platoon had obtained some vino; from where I wondered? Anyway he drank too much vino one day and hurled himself towards enemy line s. Alas a mine was his undoing and I had to write a letter to his family and advise them of his tragic death. Eventually I had a letter back from them, and I was glad that they had received my original letter. Apart from their sad comments it was clear that the soldier concerned had helped to support his family financially. This was an extra blow for them to face up to. There was no doubt many such tragic circumstances with all Services during the war.

I was now back with 'C' Company and within days we moved up through Rome to the front north of Lake Trasimeno. 'Tug' Wilson had now taken Ben Dalton's position as Company Commander and I became Second in Command of the Company.

We became involved in hill operations and the Division did very well. Our Brigade took the Corps objective well ahead of schedule, and I understood that our successful attacks led to the fall of Arezzo. We were now making good progress towards the Gothic Line in the Arezzo Sector. A damper on such operations was the fact that there were more losses in men and officers. The officers who lost their lives were 'Tiger' Brand and Murray Dixon, and another officer was badly wounded.

CHAPTER 14

The Gothic Line Including Urbino

During these recent attacks we had visits from HM the King, and General Alexander (later Field Marshal). During his visit HM the King actually watched one of our Brigades making a successful attack. Subsequently our Brigade moved to the North West of Arezzo, and we occupied ground west of 11 Brigade. This latter Brigade, especially the Camerons, had heavy casualties in their attack on a Mount Grillo. I had two platoons under command just south of Mount Grillo. We were in these positions for 48 hours and I can honestly say that I had never experienced such heavy shelling in a Company area. We were under observation the whole time, and considering the heavy shelling we were lucky in that we only had one man wounded during the whole of the 48 hours. We left there at night and we had to make four or five attempts to load the mules between the shelling bouts. It seemed that we had now reached the Gothic Line. 'C' Company had several casualties in this area. We then concentrated south of Arezzo with the rest of the Division. Divisional signs were removed, always an ominous sign, and security was tightened up 100%.

I was with a few officers who were granted leave to Rome at this time, another ominous sign. Our leave was for 48 hours and I had time to visit St. Peters in Vatican City. I remember that we were billeted with some Canadian nurses in Rome. One of the officers with me was Charles Sinclair-Thompson who commanded the Carrier Platoon at that time. He had fairly quickly arranged a date with one of the Canadian nurses, and I gave him the loan of a white shirt.

On our return from leave the Division was addressed by the present Army Commander, General Leese. I think we all felt proud when he said that there was no Infantry Division he would rather have in the 8th Army than the 4th Indian Division. We seemed to be recognised now as the Mountain Division. But he soon dispelled any rumours of our having a long rest. What he did say however, was that in our next operation he was going to give us even more mules, which means even bigger mountains! Clearly we were going to be involved in the attacks on the Gothic Line. We then did another secret move and security regulations became very tight. We were in fact in the hill country not far from Gubbio

Len Mansfield was now back with me from hospital and this was a great help. We had now endured 8 months of fighting in this country, a country which is surely one of the most difficult to fight in. It was quite possible that after the next battles we would have a rest, with the wars in Europe seeming to be coming towards some sort of end. Apparently our battalion was the oldest British Battalion in the 8th Army. Everybody feels that our job has been well done. The landing in the South of France, the

Russian drive, and the progress in Western France were at this point all very encouraging.

The landing in the South of France, the Russian drive, and the progress in Western France are very encouraging.

It was towards the end of August that the Division took part in an all out offensive on the Adriatic side of the Line in order to pierce the Gothic Line defences. Initially we had a responsibility to give protection on the left flank. Our Division was in fact, the first to break through the Line. Our 'C' Company took the brunt of the first part of the Battalion's battle, as together with the Honeys and tanks, we formed the advance guard for the Battalion. I was in command of two Platoons ordered to take the city of Urbino. John Buckeridge, who much later after the war became Colonel of the Regiment, was with me on this occasion.

The operations to take Urbino had to be attempted quickly and just before we set off in daylight two war reporters joined us. Urbino was a city of historical importance, especially as Raphael had been born there. Apparently there were approximately 20,000 civilians living there. There was no time for reconnaissance and the attack had to be made in daylight.

It was a very warm day and as we crawled through the vineyards laden with fruit we quenched our thirst with the grapes. It was very worrying however as the vineyards gave no adequate cover for our operations and the only suitable cover was to our right where the Indian infantry were operating.

As we neared the walls of the castellated city we would have expected opposition fire and shelling and mortaring, but all was quiet. Just before we clambered up the steep slopes to the outer walls, the two war reporters no doubt thought the same as I did. Either the city was empty or they did not wish to carry on fighting, the enemy that is. So the war reporters hived round the flank and I never saw them again! I supposed that they saw a story in this attack! Even after we entered the city itself it was still silent. Then all of a sudden the shuttered windows of the buildings were thrown open and cheering Italians waved with flags and handkerchiefs. The city had waited to give this welcome after the Germans had gone. To be absolutely sure we progressed through the streets as though there might be some hidden nasties, but although we were told by the locals that there might be some deserters in a building with Alsatian dogs we found nothing.

So instead of a battle I found myself sleeping in one of the best hotels in the city! It was one of the strangest operations I was ever engaged in, and came about really because the Italians were desperately anxious to save all the valuable buildings, art treasures and historical significant past. The Germans had obviously agreed to this, and later on the Mayor of the city presented to the Division in gratitude, an engraving, a copy of which I still possess, see below.

Urbino Plaque.

CHAPTER 15

Further Progress in the Gothic Line, and my Progress to Command 'D' Company, and Pian di Castello

The next day the advance continued, but the situation was now back to normal, in other words stiff resistance was to be expected. We bumped into opposition near Pieve di Cagna, one of our Honeys was knocked out by an S.P. gun, and our Company area was heavily shelled. It was on the next morning that we reached the road junction near the village itself. There was a hill feature to the west on which the enemy were resisting stiffly, and several casualties were sustained. The Carriers were involved and the bad news reached me that my friend Charles Sinclair-Thompson had lost his life. It seemed like yesterday when I had lent him a white shirt to impress his Canadian lady; that must have been his last enjoyment before this battle.

That night 'B' and 'C' Companies were involved in relief work, and shortly after this we were able to occupy Pieve di Cagna.

It has to be said that one of our Platoons had become too crowded in a stone building during the actions around Pieve di Cagna and at that time we did not know whether the enemy tanks would make another sortie towards our positions or not. The enemy had very good observation posts which quite likely were in the tower of the local church. We heard the tanks revving up and wondered what their movements would be. Fortunately for us the noise of the tank engines became fainter and we had been spared another onslaught. The enemy delaying tactics were very effective for a short time.

Another part of the Division had taken Auditore and Monte Calvo, so that the Gothic Line was now burst open.

The Battalion then had a very short respite, and then I was promoted to command 'D' Company. Major Gordon Brown, the former Company Commander had apparently been involved in a jeep accident and severely damaged his leg.

It was quite naturally a blow for me to leave 'C' Company after all that time, but even though we were in the midst of war I soon settled down with 'D' Company. After all they had been commanded by Harry Hawkes and I felt sure that they were a truly seasoned body of men, experienced in all ways. It is of course, not normally easy to settle down quickly with soldiers you don't know and they don't know you, especially during major battles. But they were a grand Company. So we battled on – 'B' Company were the Advance Guard and the objective was Pian di Castello. Unfortunately 'B' Company with tanks and jeeps had been caught in the open, as ground which was thought secure on the flank was found not to be so. Unfortunately Guy Nugent and Sergeant Bungard were killed and another officer was badly wounded. Lt. Col. Phelps sent for me and I was told to capture Pian di Castello when dusk fell. I crawled forward as best I could to Peter Cavalier who was in a hull-down carrier. Of course the information was fairly sparse and there was no time to carry out a reconnaissance first. I did learn however, that there were anti personnel mines ahead, but that no one could tell me where!

It seemed to me that my time with 'D' Company could be of short duration, but at least the Company was in good heart. So that night we moved off to the right towards Pian di Castello, and 'A' Company commanded by Hugh Sayers were going to move forward on the left.

We soon encountered schu mines and a few casualties had to be evacuated. This all took time especially in the dark. I decided that to proceed more quickly I would lead from the front with Lt. Flavell's platoon. We pushed on as quickly as we could and it was truly fortunate for us that I seemed to have found a narrow path un-mined. I see from my age old notes that we then encountered torrential rain, but we reached a position noted as Villa Bassa at first light. I put forward a patrol from here but they were fired on. We managed to contact 'A' Company and we firm-based at Villa Bassa.

My company runner named 'Peanut' Harman was with me ahead of the Company and within 24 hours we all entered Pian di Castello. It seemed likely that the Germans had retired to the village cemetery just ahead frontally. We were now being heavily shelled.

That night 'A' Company were ordered to pass through our positions and take Cemetery Hill to the north, but they had to withdraw on account of enemy fire which was heavy. Whilst I believed that one should not reinforce failure I also knew that the tanks would soon be near. This worked out well and as the tanks took out the cemetery I sent our Company, reinforced by 'A' Company, to the ridge behind the cemetery. In doing so I sent them over in small packets of about three, quickly, and they all reached the ridge successfully with Company Headquarters. We mopped up the surrendering Germans and the Padre also had a story to tell. One of our tanks had been hit and set on fire and the padre went forward to assist with any wounded. Padre Thornton was carrying a pitchfork and as he rounded a haystack he came face to face with fourteen armed German soldiers. Surprise was mutual but the pitchfork prevailed and he brought in all fourteen as prisoners. All in all we took quite a large number of prisoners, and whilst we dug in as best we could using some of the enemy positions, 'C' Company went on to attack Wood Hill, the next feature to the west. Here they had success also, and one of their young officers was awarded the MC. His platoon had been counter attacked by the enemy and he was sorely besieged. Bert Roach was the officer's name, and as he dashed between his sections he hurled grenades at the enemy. The enemy became disorganised, and despite their efforts to take the position the platoon remained intact.

Both 'C' Company and 'D' Company, remarkably, had very few casualties. However, as dusk descended I was sent two soldiers to help our position; it should not have been done. There were no more defensive positions available and I told them to dig in as soon as they could. Sadly one of the many stonks we endured happened in this period and they both lost their lives. Two 'A' Company officers were wounded.

Anyway I was so pleased at the way 'D' Company had conducted themselves, and Pian di Castello became a battle honour. I had this instinctive feeling also with 'D' Company, that our respect was mutual. They knew now that I was always determined to reach our objectives; with a minimum loss of life.

I was very pleased that eventually Sergeant Gardner was awarded the Military Medal, not only for Pian di Castello but for all his previous efforts as well. Sometimes when he and I met after the war at reunions, he would refer back to Pian di Castello and a puzzled expression would come over his face as he smoked his pipe. "How did you know how to avoid those mines on our night attack," he quizzed me. I thought a second or two and replied: "It was a lady," I replied. "A lady?" he repeated after me. "Lady Luck," I laughingly replied.

I was asked to write a spiel for the padre with his pitchfork with a view to his getting an MC, but I don't think anything ever came of it. At some stage I was awarded a mention in dispatches, but I prefer to remember the general brave work of all. Whenever I read nowadays of Self Assemblies and independence I like to recall how a Scotsman, (Tim Reilly) looked after me medically, an Irishman tried to look after my safety, especially on patrols, (Corporal Keeting); Len Mansfield who gave me such good help, (an Englishman), and Padre James, a Welshman at Monte Cassino, who risked his life to come and see me on St. David's day.

We may once have been a nation of shopkeepers, but when you have all the main elements of the UK in one posse they are the best, bar none. Anyway, I digress.

Presently we were relieved by the 1/2nd Gurkhas and we were allowed to rest for a few days. The other Brigades had more fighting before the liberation of the independent State of San Marino and I remember an orders group being held from the turreted towers of San Marino.

From the craggy hilltops and towers of San Marino I could see the hills and mountains around, and to the north the River Rubicon looked so peaceful with the sun glistening on its waters.

Anyway, 'A' company formed the advance guard as the attacks were resumed and they successfully took Trebbio. Then our Company took the Gemmiano feature. The CO came up to visit us in this position and he was well satisfied with progress so far. The next morning 'A' Company moved forward to cross the Rubicon, but their forward elements were pinned down.

Consequently that night 'A' and 'B' Companies moving together crossed the Rubicon, but the further objective of Mount Reggiano was not reached by first light so they firm based some 500 yards south of it.

The next night the same two Companies attacked again, but there was heavy enemy opposition and they ended up still short of their objective. They had suffered heavy casualties in officers and men. Our Company went up to reinforce them and we firm based in their old position.

I found the Rubicon in calm mood at that time, and we had another visit from the CO. In fact our Company jeep driver had brought him up to visit the positions. What I hadn't realised was that when they were with us Pantry had managed to quietly leave a bottle of whisky for me. It was some feat considering the time and place. 'C' Company then replaced the two forward Companies, and eventually Mount Reggiano was overcome.

I received orders to pull out that night as objectives had now been taken, and it seemed probable that we would be pulled out altogether this time from what the CO had intimated.

So quietly we moved down to the Rubicon which was now in full spate and presenting quite a contrast from when we had crossed it going forward. Then I received orders over the wireless to stay put as our Indian friends were having troubles on their front. There were naturally some short grumbles from our men, but fortunately I soon heard that we could move on as the other Battalion were now in control of their situation. Mentally I had been trying to work out the best way to recross a more angry Rubicon, and I decided to chain the soldiers by hand to hand movement with their weapons held out of the water; special care was to be taken over the short people like Peanut Harmer.

At the same time as we crossed the rough waters of the Rubicon, the Divisional positions were taken over by the 10th Indian Division. Eventually we reached the stone buildings to the rear where we were to rest until our transport arrived. Most of us slept with exhaustion and eventually at first light the lorries arrived to take us away from the Front.

Our lorries were heading south, and after we had covered about 25 miles we arrived at Perugia. Here there were reasonable billets awaiting us, and leave was shortly to be arranged.

Meanwhile the Companies were ordered to be ready for a CO's Inspection one morning, and so I inspected 'D' Company myself first with Sergeant-Major Cox. I was amazed and so impressed by the turnout after the short time since they were in action. They had been in hard battles to break the Gothic Line and apart from their own determination I knew that CSM Cox had a lot to do with such a smart turnout in such a short time. The CO carried out a thorough inspection himself, and after he had finished he spoke to myself and the CSM. He congratulated us both on the smartness of the Company, and made it clear that when the Battalion would shortly be cut back by one Company after all the casualties, 'D' Company would not be affected.

This was good news and I'm sure the word reached their ears with the morale rising accordingly. I'm sure that Harry Hawkes would have been well satisfied with the state of play.

It had been another hard battle and the rest away from the front would restore their spirits I was sure.

One day Tim Reilly was going to one of his medical centres in Assisi and he asked me if I would like to go along with him. Whilst he was dealing with his medical supplies at Assisi I took the opportunity to visit the Cathedral of St. Francis and I was struck by the silence and quietude in the precincts. The birdsong was prevalent which was so apt for this Saint. I then found a place by the waters to eat my lunch. The Italian women were busy washing their clothes in the usual way and singing pleasantly.

We drove back to Perugia as the light was fading. It had been a real breath of fresh air.

There were two other episodes that I can recall at Perugia whilst we were there. Firstly Sgt. Kemsley had become Company Quarter Sergeant – he had been in the Carriers with me before the Carrier Platoon organised the mule transport every night at Cassino – he was one of less than a handful of them who had survived that ordeal. He was now CQMS of our Company. He came to see me one morning to tell me that he had received news from home regarding his marriage, which by all accounts needed sorting out. After all he had been through in battle this was the last thing that he needed. I discussed it with the CO and I am happy to say that compassionate leave was arranged for him. I hope that he did save his marriage; in fact our paths did not cross again so I do not know how he fared at that time. Of course this left a vacancy for the position of CQMS, and I am glad to say that Sgt. Gardner MM was promoted to this position.

The other small incident occurred when I had an evening meal with Doc Tim Reilly at the Officers Club in Perugia. It had been a pleasant evening with the meal and wine when just before we were leaving, an Italian lady placed her hand on my shoulder. She spoke in Italian of course, but I could not grasp what she had said. Fortunately the Doc had apparently understood. "She said that you were very young to be a Major." The Doc then said to her without waiting for me, "That's because he is a brave man." The lady went on her way as I scolded the Doc for his kind words. By that time in the war I felt sure there were a number of officers who were Majors at the age of 24. After a short time we moved from Perugia to Orvieto, famed for its wines and an impressive cathedral. At Orvieto we occupied an Italian barracks, and parties of men were sent on leave from here.

Meanwhile we knew that the infantry Companies were to be reorganised into three Companies following Lt.Col. Phelps's advance warning, and 'A' and 'B' Companies were amalgamated and became known as 'B' Company, whilst 'C' Company remained as 'C' Company. 'D' Company became known as 'A' Company. Although I was the junior Major I remained in command of 'D' Company, (now 'A' Company).

Quite confusing!

After a few days at Orvieto I set out on seven days leave to Rome accompanied by Hugh Sayers and Ken Milne, the latter being Intelligence Officer. However we were recalled after 48 hours! The Battalion moved by road right down to Taranto – at that time Ken Milne went into hospital with jaundice, and Norman Ralph became Intelligence Officer instead.

It was obvious that we were soon to leave Italy, land of rivers and mountains, and I wondered what was in store for us next.

Greece was the answer to that, the Brigade being destined for Salonika. It was hoped that the landing would be unopposed, and our intended role was 'internal security'.

But things never turn out as planned and we knew that at present the country was very unstable in many ways. We just had to wait and see.

CHAPTER 16

A Grecian Odyssey

In earlier days of the war the Greeks had to defend their land against the Italian invasion; this they did heroically. Hitler had to intervene to assist the Italians, and the Germans crossed the Greco-Bulgarian frontier, after which their panzer columns were soon in Athens. Thus Greece passed to German control and the Bulgarians took over much of Macedonia. In fact the people in Macedonia were harshly treated and the Germans generally devastated the rest of Greece; thousands of villages were destroyed and many Greeks were either shot or imprisoned, schools were closed and the press were made non effective. There was a serious famine in the land and guerrilla groups formed in the mountains. Unfortunately some of these local groups were from left wing groups and some were from the right wing. The Communist groups were quite strong, and their armed forces were known as ELAS. Generally they ignored their King who was based in Cairo. He was supported by the group named EDES. There was therefore hostility between ELAS and EDES, and the former had established relationships with President Tito of Yugoslavia. So this very volatile situation had to be dealt with by a tentative agreement between the Greek factions and the acceptance of Allied forces as the Germans retreated northwards. They adopted a policy of scorched earth as they withdrew. The farms were destroyed, bridges blown and so on. It was not surprising that when the British arrived in Athens they had a very warm welcome. The British Commander was Lt. General Scobie.

We were still a part of 7th Indian Brigade in the 4th Indian Division and our destination was to be Macedonia. This meant that we had a sea voyage to Salonika. 5th Indian Brigade would be in the Athens area, and the 11th Indian would be in the Peloponnese. We ourselves hoped that our landing would be unopposed and we were informed that our role was 'internal security.' However we were also told that the situation was very unstable there.

The Battalion Orders Group of which I was a member, proceeded by a Canadian Naval vessel named 'The Prince Henry' to Athens for orders from the Brigade Commander of the Parachute Brigade. We worked under this Brigade Commander for this part of the operations. The remainder of the Battalion proceeded with their vehicles on Landing Ships Tanks (LSTs) and we were to rejoin them at sea. In Athens all points were tied up and it was confirmed to us that the Germans had now left Salonika. Before they evacuated Salonika the Germans had apparently carried out extensive demolitions in the dock area. During our short stay in Athens I managed to visit the Acropolis, but I could also see demonstrations indicating political tensions in the area. A destroyer, HMS Exmoor (Hunt Class) took us to rejoin our main convoy. It was quite a tricky operation climbing the rope ladder of the LST in a turbulent sea! I was Officer

Commanding troops on our LST and operations went very smoothly to start with. The original plan had been to beach near Cape Kara in view of the damage to the quaysides in Salonika, but this was reversed and the final plan was to go right into Salonika. There was considerable delay in the Gulf of Salonika as we were held up by magnetic and acoustic sea mines. The Germans had made a very thorough job of it. It so happened that we had a couple of war reporters on board, shades of Urbino, and they harassed me quite a bit over the delay. They were no doubt keen to get ashore for their storylines, and I had to explain patiently the reasons for the delay, and why the food consisted of hard tack for the most part.

Anyway, after a short distance we were transferred to motor gunboats and other landing craft. The Naval Officer on my vessel was morally very cheering with his offer of hot coffee, but he pointed out that it was the worst Gulf they had ever come across for the density of mines. Eventually we came right into the port without casualties thanks to the Royal Navy. Before I left our LST, a Greek naval Officer presented to me a Greek puppy, a Red Setter. I decided that the Company could keep it for now. The puppy was named 'Whisky.'

The German demolition units had destroyed the dock installations so that the port was unusable, but the water, electricity and other supplies were usable. The Brigade came ashore, it was now 12th November. I still remember that the first Greek civilian I met was a middle aged lady who expressed her gratitude for our presence. Our Battalion took over guard duties on vulnerable points (VPs), but I soon found out that ELAS soldiers were about the area. The next day I took part, with a detachment of the now called 'A' Company, in a big procession for the arrival of representatives of the Greek national government and the presence of Greek military governors. The ELAS had representatives in this procession, and although they seemed to tolerate us they were not prepared to cooperate in the rehabilitation of Macedonia. They were more concerned in defeating the Security Battalions at places inland.

A few days later Major Ben Dalton returned to the Battalion from his Staff Course, and he took over 'A' Company at that time and I reverted to Second in Command. My Captaincy was now substantive and it seemed not unlikely that I would be back to Major before too long. I take this opportunity to say that my brother Ronnie had become a Major in the Indian Army in India a while back, and this was good news for the family at home. My sister Edna was serving with the WVS at the time, and no doubt she was kept busy as well.

We were in good billets in Salonika, the owners of the property where we were billeted were quite friendly and as the wintry weather was now upon us, they let us have some of their fuel at a fair price.

By mid November there was more trouble with ELAS in Salonika. It was reported that ELAS were making unauthorised arrests including some Greek Reserve Officers who might well be called up by the Provisional Government. At the same time some interpreters were being intimidated and told to stop their employment. We were ordered to reform the Salonika National Guard and disarm the ELAS from December 10th.

Meanwhile the 5th Indian Brigade were in the Athens area, and on December 3rd the police opened fire on left wing demonstrators in Athens. ELAS armed forces were soon on the streets of Athens and they did in fact surround the British Headquarters in the Grand Bretagne Hotel. There were few British Forces in Athens at that time. Some British Forces were flown in and the 5th Indian Brigade helped to defend the port of Piraeus. Sea communications were essential and the protection of the port was very important.

It has to be realised that at least 70,000 men were in the ELAS military in this part of Greece, and they were well trained. They were well armed and the position was tense. In fact there was some fierce fighting in and around Athens during December.

The situation in and around Salonika had now become very tense, and Christmas was a worrying time. We did not want to be involved in any local quarrels, and the troops of 7th Indian Brigade were scattered around Macedonia.

In fact our stay in Salonika had been pleasant in some ways, and I was welcomed into one house where a Professor lived with his daughter. They tried to teach me the language of Greek. What an undertaking! Although I could remember a Classics master encouraging me in that direction, and the daughter was very pleasant too!

By the 17th December we were reinforced and we were able to move to Drama to relieve the Paratroops and Commandos there. But the situation throughout the country was becoming worse. The Battalion was then moved to Kavalla on the seafront. At Drama we had been billeted in the Tobacco Research Institute just outside the town. At Kavalla our Company was part of a strong force stationed at Kavalla airfield. From a military point of view it was not a healthy situation, the ELAS were on the surrounding hills; it had also become very cold!

There was heavy fighting in Athens and it was possible that the balloon would go up where we were!

The wintry conditions were so severe that the little dog Whisky did not survive in spite of the attention he received.

A cruiser HMS Caledon was lying off shore at Kavalla; one day I had a very pleasant lunch aboard ship, and they were a comforting presence.

Eventually around Christmas time Winston Churchill and Field Marshall Alexander arrived in Athens and there was a conference with important Greek officials, including the main Archbishop. In early January the ELAS started to withdraw from Athens, there had been reinforcements strengthening the British force, and the Communist aims of ELAS had been thwarted. The 5th Indian Brigade were now able to effectively help the sick, and wounded and poverty stricken Athenians. It was hoped that 7th Indian Brigade would now be able to fan out and bring aid and succour to Northern Macedonia. The arrival of two British Divisions in Southern Greece would hopefully now enable us to carry out this work.

As regards the 11th Indian Brigade, their destination at the start of the campaign had been the Peloponnese where there was less tension at that time. This Brigade had been taken over by Brigadier Hunt who after the war was in charge of the party of climbers who conquered Mount Everest at the time of the Coronation.

There were armed ELAS in Patras, and the same difficulties over handing over arms occurred there.

Eventually a truce was signed in Athens and the 11th Indian Brigade after hardships reached Missolonghi and the Gulf of Corinth. It had been a very difficult time for the whole Division and it was now hoped that our Brigade would be able to fan out from Salonika. Once a place had been cleared the Greek National Guard moved in.

Before long I had to take an advance guard from our Company to Kilkis which was very much an ELAS stronghold. I had some Carriers with me and some of our Company infantry, but I anticipated that there might be trouble as we made our way to Kilkis. Eventually I met the civil and ELAS powers and reassured them of our presence. However, they were not prepared for us to take over their quarters, but after bluffing that there were tanks on the way, some Army barracks on the perimeter were pointed out to me and they seemed ideal for our surveillance operations. The Greek National Guard would eventually take over from us we hoped. So another hurdle had been overcome but the public utilities needed help to make them operative again. Eventually Ben Dalton arrived with the rest of the force and we began to settle in.

One day I was asked to go into the town and see if I could obtain any booze as we had none at all. I visited several of the local bars and eventually found one that seemed to approve of our presence. Unfortunately the only supply they could provide was Cherry Brandy! I tried one or two glasses and decided that it would have to do. In fact the efforts were quite appreciated, especially as apparently I had become somewhat over indulgent myself!

The company was eventually back in Drama and Ben Dalton had now gone on a Staff College Course, so I was re-promoted to Major again.

Field Marshall Auchinleck was at this time C in C Indian Army and he was about to pay a visit to 4th Indian Division. Lt. Col. Phelps was away on leave and the Battalion was being commanded by Major Shinkwin. I was told to command the Guard of Honour at Kavalla Airfield as the Auk came off his plane, and he was to meet also Major Shinkwin, RSM Phillips and others, including all of the Company. It all went off very well and I was happy that RSM Phillips and CSM Cox had the opportunity to meet Field Marshall Auchinleck. They had both served the Battalion well.

The Battalion had now been made up to four rifle Companies again, and there was a period of fanning out in Macedonia, with the Greek National Guard taking over the cleared locations as the ELAS were disarmed.

I then had orders to take the Company to Kavalla, and two Platoons were stationed there not far from Brigade Headquarters. The 3rd Platoon was stationed on the island of Thasos, to be reached only by caique! Also there was an officers' billet near the port. It was a pleasant time for us. Most of the work was operational, disarming various guerrilla parties and allowing the Greek National Guard to take over their own Greeks and their positions.

It was also necessary to search the villages for arms which was not an easy task. It usually meant having a greasy meal with the village mayor whilst the search was going on. When it was possible to decide if the village was reasonably clear, the *United Nations Relief and Rehabilitation Administration* (UNRRA) would step in with food and medical supplies. The Americans saw to this and I had a very pleasant working relationship with an American nurse who was helping to oversee the UNRRA work. I also had a very good interpreter, Paul Kelras by name. It was only practical to visit Thasos occasionally, but there were friendly football matches with the locals. Also Brigade Headquarters were very hospitable and I had pleasant times there as well. Pantry still drove me around in the Company jeep and with Betty Edmunds my American friend, the three of us found an idyllic beach not far from the Turkish border. The waters were now warming up.

And then one day just before we left Kavalla, the day we had all been waiting for arrived – VE Day! It so happened that the Company had arranged a dance that evening and it all went with a swing! It was hard to believe in this corner of the world that the war in Europe was over at last. There were many celebrations with the Greeks as well; Greece had stood side by side with Great Britain in defence of democracy in 1941 when all had seemed nearly lost.

Before we left Kavalla there was a visiting ENSA troop and they were very good. Such an isolated place to come to, strangely enough the lady singer who had all the lads singing lustily came from Swansea; a small world?

There was then a Company changeover and 'D' Company moved back to Drama, our position in Kavalla being taken over by John Buckeridge and his Company. Battalion headquarters was still ensconced at Drama, situated in the Tobacco Research Institute, our former billet in more serious times. The rest of the Battalion were billeted in the adjoining barracks. Most of our work was of an operational nature but plenty of opportunity existed for recreational training, and in spite of the intense heat there was cricket, football and a Battalion Sports Day. Bathing parties were also sent to Kavalla and they used the suitable beaches there.

We had suitable services of Thanksgiving for the end of the European war. Apparently there was to be a General Election in the UK and the Service vote would no doubt be important. Lecturers from the Educational Army Units came, and although as an officer I would on no account interfere with a soldier's political views, I thought there were times when the lecturers were slightly biased in their talks. Rumours seemed to exist that if the men voted for Labour they might get their demob earlier. This was absurd really, I've no doubt that detailed plans could not be suddenly overturned anyway. There were also thoughts that we might at some stage be shipped to the Far East war against Japan, certainly this was much in the minds of the Americans.

In July the Battalion was again concentrated in Salonika. Apparently we were approaching the time when the British Units such as ourselves would be leaving the famous 4th Indian Division. For the time being our places were to be taken by the Lovat Scouts and the 2nd Battalion Highland Light Infantry.

There was a big farewell parade; we had come to admire all the fighting skills of the Indians, the Gurkhas, Punjabis, Sikhs and all the others. Now it was a joyous time tinged with sadness in the farewell.

The Battalions were to be flown from Salonika to Klagenfurt in Austria. It was during this move that I was suddenly informed that I was going on leave to the UK, which was great news!

I thought of all that had happened to us since I had been in the UK and at home with my family. The general news of the war was now good. I had also received several pieces of pleasant news about family and friends. Jack eventually managed to return to England from North Africa, and had a position with the Army Kinema Corporation. This was good news as he had always been interested in the ins and outs of cinema. I remember that he had an office in Dover Street at one time, and his driver one day turned out to be an aunt of mine, Aunt Gladys who was doing her bit for the war effort as an ATS driver. After they had chatted for a while they realised that I was the nephew! I had also received letters from time to time from Bobby Gibb who lived in Swansea. He had been on the same troopship as me when we went abroad.

As I have already said my brother Ronnie had done well in the Indian Army in India. It was in India that he met his future wife Pam, and they were happily married for many years, and with family.

I should like to refer to 'D' Company Headquarters again. Harry Hawkes had a fine Company when I had to take it over in the midst of battle, and the Company headquarters were very much a part of the Unit. Apart from CSM Cox and CQMS Gardner, there was Pantry (Driver), Bishop (Stores), Peanut Harmer (Company Runner), Plutheroe (Company Clerk, eventually he became Battalion Orderly Sergeant, most of the time he was known as Pluto!).

There were also the signallers and stretcher bearers who did such a splendid job. By the time I was due to go on leave to the UK, Len Mansfield had already left for England. What a tower of strength he had been. I bade a temporary farewell to the CO, the Adjutant and others. I say temporary as I had decided to stay on for a limited time only.

Before leaving Salonika I received the pleasant news that my father had been honoured with an OBE. I am sure that it was well deserved after all his work around the docks in all sorts of weather, and his knowledge of shipping and his ability to get on with all sorts of people whoever they were.

Guard of Honour for visit of General Auchinleck (later Field Marshall) to Kavalla Airfield. He was C-in-C India at the time. Auchinleck is talking to CSM Cox.

Auchinleck and RSM Philips.

'D' Company at Kavalla 1945. The author is in the front.

Roy Rees meeting General Auchinleck at Kavalla.

Roy Rees and Major Shinkwin with General Auchinleck.

Roy Rees and Captain Norman Ralph during a visit to the Parthenon in Athens.

Greece VE Day 1945. Parade led by author.

VE Day Service, Greece 1945. Author standing on extreme left.

Len Mansfield (batman), Greece January 1945.

CHAPTER 17

Travels to the UK for leave and the joys of seeing relatives and friends again

It was to be the last time that we would proudly wear the Red Eagle Divisional sign and all that meant. On our return from leave we would no doubt proudly wear the Mailed Fist of the 6th Armoured Division.

A great character of the battalion was Jim (Plugger) Day, and it so happened that he was also going on leave. He knew great chunks of the history of the regiment, and, firstly as the Quartermaster and then as Support Company Commander, he had been a comforting presence during the battles.

We travelled by LST to Athens from Salonica; strangely it was the same LST that had transported us to Salonica in the first place. There was a few days wait in Athens where we caught up with Harry Hawke and 'Goldie' Goldsmith, who were returning to the area we had come from.

I then flew to Foggia in Italy. Plugger was supposed to be flying over the following day but we did not meet up again. From Foggia I travelled by train to Naples. Then there was a train journey to Milan. I did in fact have two pleasant days in Milan.

The hotel near the railway station was very comfortable, and I managed to visit the Cathedral, and see some opera at La Scala, the theatre was already up and running, Rigoletto I remember.

Eventually it was time to board our train at Milan station. I must have drawn the short straw as I was instructed to be OC the train. It was not unnatural that those going home on leave were in cheerful mood, but I did notice the message had been chalked on the front of the train saying: 'Look out Lady Astor here we come'. Lady Astor had made some speech in Parliament which I believe suggested that perhaps the pay for soldiers in Italy could be reduced, the saved monies no doubt to go to some other worthy cause. If you have read my book so far you will realise how unpopular and unjust such an action would have been for the fighting soldiers in Italy. Perhaps this is a suitable point to mention that a chap at Ellesmere in my time there, his name was Blunt, received a VC for his work and brave exploits in the Italian battles. The same situation arose also in Burma who became known as 'The Forgotten Army' but their deeds there also spoke for themselves.

Another incident that I had to deal with on this particular train was in connection with someone who wrote under the Press name of Cassandra. I think it was the chap who eventually had a senior appointment in the Wilson Cabinet. Anyway, he came into my compartment complaining about poor travelling arrangements for the soldiers. Having already been around the carriages I suppose he was really right but I knew that the soldiers were not complaining, I think he just liked to stir things up. I happened to have some whiskey in my kit and he accepted a drink from me so I hope that he did not make any unfavourable report in his newspaper!

This was in fact, the first train to leave Milan for the Channel Ports and there had been quite a send off. We travelled through Switzerland and France. We then travelled across the Straits by a channel steamer. I seem to remember that the Customs officials at the UK port were somewhat officious in all the circumstances, and with persuasion I did manage eventually to get them to allow me through with a fairly ordinary camera. Then I was on my way to Paddington to catch the train to Wales, having already wired through the expected time of arrival.

It was like old times travelling down to South Wales by train, and the countryside was the summer green that I remembered so well. The same stops on the railway at Reading, Swindon, Newport, Cardiff, and then the other stations to Swansea. As the train slowly entered the station I thought at last I've made it. And there they were on the platform, were my parents, my sister Edna and her husband Colin and various aunts. My brother Ronnie and his wife were, of course, still in India. My father had already grabbed my valise and was heading off to the car. A quick journey to the area known as Sketty and we reached the front door of my parents home. There was a welcome home sign at the entrance door. Some of the time I spent with my parents and some of the time with my sister and her husband. The latter two had now moved down to a village called Horton in the Gower Peninsular by the sea. It was now August and as I walked along the cliff paths the old memories of past times came back to me. The times when we were kids adventuring along the beaches and sea. Some had not survived the war, but it was clear to me that apart from fighting for other countries independence, it was these shores that surrounded the British Isles that we had fought for. The seas and cliffs and all the land within had been in jeopardy, but we had kept the faith.

And then one day when I was in Swansea the news came through about the atom bombs on Japan. Such terrifying effects, and yet the world war was now over. I would not have to go to Japan after all, but we soon learnt of the terrible times the Service personnel had experienced out East.

Nevertheless there were VJ parties in the locality and my parents duly obliged with a party in their home. One of the highlights of this party was the memory of my Aunt trying to hit the middle ceiling light with her foot, and then my father who was a short man then tried himself. By this time my mother intervened in protestation, but she was happy nevertheless.

I soon had to say farewell and I had a smooth journey back to Paddington. At Victoria I joined up with colleagues who were also going back to join the Battalion in Austria.

At this stage I must mention that before I left Victoria I had time to visit my old friend Jack and his wife Joyce and to see their new baby daughter. The baby's name was Trudy and I was the godfather for her. It was an occasion of much happiness, and Jack did in fact return with me to Victoria to see me off with the lads, which was very kind of him.

CHAPTER 18

Post War in Austria, Italy and Germany

W e did not arrive at Folkestone until midnight, so we were accommodated overnight in the Royal Pavilion Hotel. We were just about to get on board the next morning when the sailing was cancelled due to rough weather. So we had a further day in Folkestone before we actually set sail and duly arrived in Calais. There was then a five day road journey to Villach in Austria. We travelled via Sedan, Luxembourg, Mainz, Ulm and Mannheim. This meant passing through Ober-Ammergau, Innsbruck, the Brenner Pass and then into Northern Italy and back to Austria! It was a most interesting journey and eventually we rejoined the Battalion a few miles from Klagenfurt the same day.

The CO was still Lt. Col. Phelps and he was particularly pleased to see me, as several of our young officers had been posted to the Far East and there were also several on leave.

I took over 'D' Company again. The countryside was so very pleasant, and I found myself living in a Schloss with the owners who were a Count and Countess. Our Company was stationed in a village on its own. The letter to my parents describing all this was dated 31st August and they received it on 4th September. Letters were now more speedily received and I was able to thank my parents for such a wonderful leave.

We soon moved to Verona as part of the 6th Armoured Division and the Battalion occupied a barracks nearby. The officer's quarters were in a house in Verona, but were soon transferred to billets near the barracks.

In mid September I received orders to carry out a reconnaissance in Germany, travelling to Ulm on the Danube. The intention was to set up a transit camp for personnel travelling home on leave and for those returning from leave to their units. Various units in the Divisions were to take it in turns to run these camps and my Company was considered suitable as it had a full strength of officers at that time.

The journey would encompass three countries, namely Italy Austria and Germany. On the reconnaissance I took with me a driver, (alas Pantry had already left), Len Mansfield and CQMS Gardner. There were many times later when Tommy Gardner recalled that I told him that we were going to Germany as though it was just up the road!

Ulm was in the American zone and they looked after me very well. I was shown the barracks that the soldiers would occupy, and their quarters, also the kitchens and dining areas. The Americans had already arranged some quarters for me and the officers, although it did seem that at least part of a German family were still living there. "Then you must have a car and interpreter," the American guide said. They would see to this also. It was no doubt very helpful of our Allies, but I did think that perhaps our commanders would not have been quite so ruthless in their requisitioning powers.

Anyway, we had a lovely run back through the same country that I had come up through on my way back from leave. I arrived back in Verona but we would have to move up to Ulm in two days time. Unfortunately, but fortunately for him, Len Mansfield had to be attached to another company pending his forthcoming release. This could come at any time. A chap by the name of West took his place. West had already taken on the batman's role when Len Mansfield had been in hospital, but the latter was a sad loss. I'm sure he was eager to see his family again.

Our company moved up to Ulm without mishap and it seemed strange that we would be hundreds of miles away from the rest of the Battalion for a few weeks. The company would be esconced in the same quarters as the transitory soldiers and 'D' Company would have to ensure the cleanliness of the billets and the standard of food and comfort for the visitors.

I showed the officers where we would put our heads at night and introduced them to the Germans in residence there. I felt a slight sense of resentment shown by the few Germans there of both sexes, although they were obviously starting up business again, whatever that was.

Soon the daily routine fell into order, and once the overnight stay of the lorry convoy was on its way again there was time for leisure and goodwill with the Americans. I visited the cathedral with its tall spire and I was glad to see that it seemed undamaged from air raids. The German interpreter was of great help, and I was taken to the Dachau concentration camp. It was a very sad experience and what went on there was something that should never have been allowed to happen. As fighting soldiers we had never heard of these camps, and it was a dreadful indictment of mankind.

One evening I invited the few Germans living in the house to share an evening meal with us. I invited the interpreter as well as I thought it would ease the flow of conversation. This turned out not to be a good idea. At first all was well with polite conversation, but there came a moment when speaking in their own language that the interpreter became involved in a somewhat heated conversation with a male German resident. I did not know what this was about, but if I had to make a guess it could well have been that the few residents resented the German interpreter helping the former enemy as he had been doing. Anyway I never did try this again, I just carried on with my job.

The time came to hand over our duties at Ulm and we rejoined the rest of the Battalion in Verona.

We managed to carry out a certain amount of training and wireless equipment was now more up to date. For leisure I have to state that there were some very fine Austrian horses stabled in the area. It was also the case that Lt. Col. Phelps was keen on horse riding activity, even though he needed a short ladder to mount his steed in view of his height. This was a form of leisure that I was not particularly looking forward to; I had never ridden a horse before. I was allotted to a horse that bore the name of 'Phantom.'

The dictionary generally refers to 'phantom' as a spirit or apparition, or giving an illusionary appearance. Perhaps one associates a phantom ship with the Flying Dutchman; Phantom was certainly a flying horse alright, and after a few rides we began to understand each other. Of course when we were nearing the stables on the return to base he recognised the terrain and put a spurt on, if he could! Presently it was decided to have a horse paper chase, there being no hounds. I can't say that I was looking forward to this, especially the jumps over the hedges as there was a certain amount of barbed wire around. Anyway Phantom jumped the hedges with aplomb but at the same time he was beginning to lag behind the field. Suddenly he veered off from the paper trail and through some tree groves. This gave him a certain amount of cover as I watched the other side of the grove as the other horses thundered back towards the base. As though he had done this short cut before, Phantom calmly joined the final gallop and trot with the others. Nuff said!

Evening leisure was partly taken up with playing Bridge, but then one morning I was sent for by the CO. Apparently an Officers' Club had opened in Verona and we had been asked to support it, and there would be suitably vetted Signorinas for us to chat to, with refreshments and dancing as well. In other words the CO did not wish to go, but a few of us were asked to show the flag in spite of our weakness with the Italian language.

So the appointed evening arrived and we sallied forth into the historic city of Verona. There were thankfully other Army personnel besides us at the club which had quite a pleasant ambiance. After having a drink of vino and some sandwiches I had a look into a large room with a dance floor, and with some old waltzes and foxtrots emanating from an old wind up record player.

I asked one of the Italian ladies present for a dance, and I quickly found out that she spoke very good English which was helpful. She lived with her family in Verona and over time she showed me the various historical places in the city and by the river. I also visited her family in their home and they were very friendly. It was only when they talked about the shelling and the bombing of the city that they naturally became very sad. Later on in life I was able to reciprocate Fiorella's kindness when she visited London and I showed her some of our famous places in the capital.

There was one occasion at our quarters in Verona when a member of another company committed suicide. I had to conduct a Court of Enquiry, presumably because I was not part of this particular company. It certainly wasn't easy to find out why this sad event had taken place, but there seemed to have been a problem with his cleanliness. Maybe he had been mercilessly twigged about this but nothing was proven. I ensured that he had a proper military funeral which I attended.

Christmas came upon us and I helped to decorate the dining messes. Part of the entertainment was a football match between the Officers and the Sergeants although it was not taken too seriously, probably just as well in the festive season!

In February I went to a Ski Centre that had been set up in the Dolomites for training, and I think that we all felt that the mountain training was like old times. I don't know why but there were several soldiers on a charge each morning for being late on early parade. I was in the Company office one morning wondering why this should occur, when Ben Dalton suddenly walked in. He had come up to the Dolomites to help out with the training. I explained that all was well, and then I told him about how some in the mornings had difficulty in being punctual for first parade. Anyway, the position in this respect did not improve even when Ben was helping to diagnose the problem. I don't recall that we ever did resolve this. They had been first class on the exercises. Perhaps it was the mountain air in conjunction with what was known as being demob happy!

We then left Verona and moved up to Lake Garda where it was very pleasant. We were actually stationed on the lakeside itself at Gardone Riviera in the hotel premises formerly occupied by Germans who had been convalescing there. Battalion Headquarters were housed in the Grand Hotel and my company was billeted in the Savoy Hotel on the lakeside. There was an officers mess in a villa on the hillside overlooking the lake. It was possible to keep up a degree of training and apart from marches and physical exercises there was a shooting range. In addition, in the past, the Battalion had been quite a force at hockey. So the football pitch was used for football and hockey. I did try the latter game which I had never played before, but it seemed fairly hazardous with hockey sticks waving about and the ball being extremely hard! I suppose there were other people like me playing who had never played before and had little knowledge of the laws of the game.

On the rifle range I sometimes came across a soldier who explained his poor results on the rifle, and they would suggest that the rifle should be given to the armourer for zeroing. Now I was only an average shot myself but if I obtained a reasonable result with their rifle I realised that there was nothing wrong with the weapon!

By now the Battalion Commander was able to have out from the UK his wife together with his two young children, and he had a residence nearer the lake. There was one occasion at this station when a fire broke out in the Grand Hotel; this was in the early morning before I would normally get up. It was the same for all of course. With the assistance of the Brescia Fire Brigade the fire was eventually put out, but I don't know what caused this incident.

The adjutant was now Norman Ralph who had taken over from George Harper. Once or twice he asked me if I would handle a court martial as President in Verona. They were not cases that had anything to do with any of our own troops. I found the military law quite interesting and the cases I dealt with were open and shut cases. On one occasion Ben Dalton came with me to learn the ropes of these proceedings. I remember a swish lunch had been laid on for us, I don't know why, but the laid table was so impressive that cameras came out to record this gastronomic feast. Our work on the court martials finished before luncheon.

The Welch Regiment had a Battalion stationed at Sirmione just down the lake from us. Sirmione was a very attractive lakeside spot and some of their officers came over to dine with us one evening. Before they left our officers gave a rendering of the regimental marching song 'Sussex by the Sea'. With my experience of Wales I felt that this would not go unanswered. I was right! The Welch responded with singing voices of quality with typical Welsh songs. Anyway a good time was had by all. Later on I was invited to the Welch mess for an evening meal on St. David's Day and I accepted. When the meal was drawing to a close a waiter came in carrying a plate full of raw leeks. Each officer then ate a leek and followed it up with a song. I was becoming rather worried about this as I had not a good singing voice and I did not relish the thought of eating a raw leek! The officer looking after me as a guest was sitting by me. "Don't worry," he said quietly, "Guests are not expected to perform this ritual." I breathed a sigh of relief and ate my cheese with more confidence!

It was of course not likely that we would stay in this idyllic place forever, and eventually we moved to Trieste, firstly in a tented camp on the outskirts of the port. Our main duties here were to keep the peace, as Tito of Yugoslavia was putting pressure on the Allies for Trieste to become part of Yugoslavia. We had to go into the port on several occasions to help keep the peace. We were transferred to some barracks near Trieste, and the port eventually became part of Italy. There were some good restaurants in Trieste and we had been told that the Triestine ladies were very striking, perhaps a mixture of the Mediterranean and Slav regions.

Blackie, still our Quartermaster, had been in charge of the Battalion football side, and he asked me if I would take over this duty, which I did. There were some good players in the 6th Armoured Division at that time, including Tom Finney the famous England and Preston player, and a noted amateur at that time was Pawson. Although we did not possess such stars in our Battalion side then, one or two such as Bashford and Wright were a great asset to our side. Wright was in my company and at the time of this incident we had a forthcoming big match. I was therefore quite concerned one morning when I saw that Wright was on a charge. It seemed that he had been on a night out and he had been spotted on his return urinating on some well kept grass. My mind quickly noted that if he was reprimanded with 7 days confinement to barracks he would miss the all important game. Perhaps I was wrong but I decided to admonish him which meant he could play in the game. This is what I did and for once my admonishment was quite severe. I had realised from an earlier staff concert that when an impersonation of me was done I gave the impression that at the end of ticking off a person on company parade/detail, I gave the punishment in milder terms, in the circumstances the punishment then surprised the guilty soldier! In Wright's case I did the opposite!

The CO of the Battalion was now Lt. Col. Ashworth and Trieste was to be my last posting. I seem to remember being taken into Trieste for a dinner with the CO and John Buckeridge, and then I had a farewell dinner with some of my officer friends who were available at the time. You will see that Arthur Jones who was in charge of the Mess at that time, produced a so-called funny menu and some of those present have signed the reverse of the said menu.

I was then on my way home.

Trieste
Demonstration.

The author leading The Royal Sussex Regiment just behind the Camerons.

Roy Rees with Kit Norton at Lake Garda.

Lt Col Phelps, Ben Dalton and John Buckeridge on a gondola in Venice.

1st BN THE ROYAL SUSSEX REGT.

IN HONOUR OF THE DEPARTURE OF MAJOR REES SAHIB

S P E C I A L   M E N U

Hors d'Oeuvres à la Rees
(niente shell-fish)

Poison? (Possibly Poisson?)
Solée dorée

Chop de Porc Charentiere
(Pork chop to Roysie)

Pommes Françaises
Tomatoes grillé
Petits Pois
(Peas to You)

Coup glacé Melba
Pears

Deadly Cigars !!!!
Café
(niente milk - so you've had white)

S.O.Y.C. !!!!

God bless - all the best

Farewell dinner to Roy Rees.

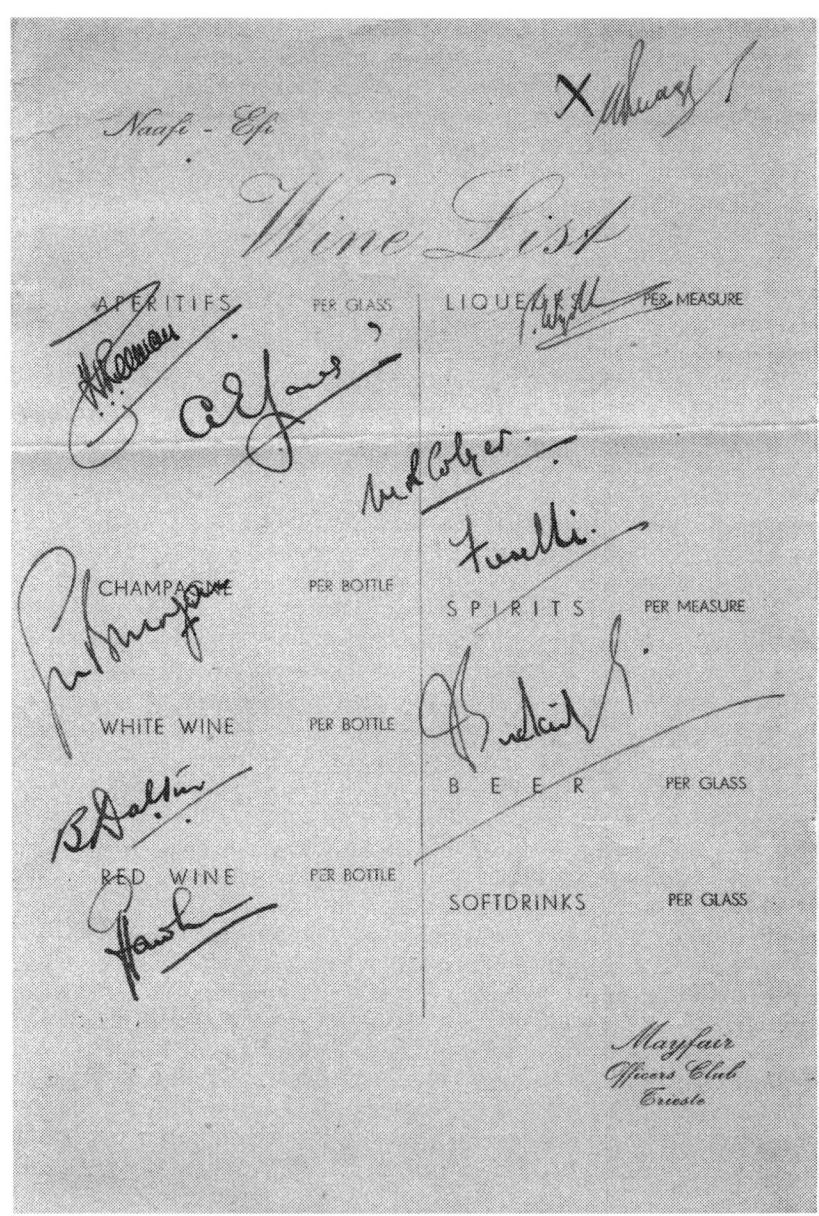

The reverse of the dinner menu was signed by the officers present as a memento.

CHAPTER 19

Reflections

The Royal Sussex Regiment was actually founded in Ireland, and its first Commanding Officer was Arthur Chichester the 3rd Earl of Donegal. The 35th of Foot was formed in the early part of the 18th century. Later on the Regiment moved to England. Historically the Officers were allowed to drink the Monarch's health without rising. The preferred reason for this was the Regiment's activity at that time, being under naval command.

It was at the Battle of Quebec in Canada that the Regiment under General Wolfe achieved victory over the French. General Wolfe alas died in these battles, but the 35th Foot were successful in overcoming the Royal Rousillon Regiment and the plume of this French Regiment has since always formed part of the Royal Sussex Regiment cap badge.

Moving forward over the centuries, the Royal Sussex Regiment with its many Battalions were very prominent in both world wars on active service.

So when the powers that be decided after World War II to reduce infantry numbers drastically, in spite of Korea where some of our men were involved, it was a great disappointment that the Royal Sussex Regiment ceased as such to be an active Regiment, but was formed into integrated units with other Home Counties regiments under a different title.

However the Royal Sussex Regiment is still very active with its Association and branches of the Association throughout Sussex and London.

Historically too, there has been a link for some time with the House of Orange, usually as a sports day.

Some years later I attended the laying up of the Colours in Chichester Cathedral, and met many old friends at that time.

The Royal Sussex have a well known Regimental marching song – 'Sussex by the Sea'. It is now heartily sung at regular reunions and other suitable occasions. To give the reader a feel of this, one of the verses is as follows:

And when you go to Sussex
Whoever you may be
You may tell them all
That we stand or fall
For Sussex by the sea!

As an appendage of so called verse I also attach at the end of the chapter some words that rhyme that reflected at the time the feelings of what had been said in the UK about the stiff battles in Italy. It is not my composition, but it is sung to the tune of 'Lily Marlene'.

I have mentioned the name of Brigadier Hunt elsewhere in this book; in later life he wrote a book called 'Meeting People' because there is an inference that meeting people is what life is all about. There is a large measure of truth in this. It was my privi-

```
"D" DAY DODGERS.
----------O---------

We're the D Day dodgers out in Italy,
Always on the Vino, always on the spree,
Eighth Army Skivvies and the Yanks,
We live in Rome and dodge the Tanks,
For we're the D day dodgers.

Naples and Cassino we've taken in our stride,
We did'nt go to fight there, just went for a ride,
Anzio and Sangro, we're OK.
And to us just a holiday,
Fo r we're the D day lodgers out here in Italy.

Once we had a big fright we were going home,
Back to dear old Blighty never more to roam,
Then someone whispered in France you will fight,
We said alright we'll just sit tight,
For we're the D day dodgers out here in Italy.

On the way to Florence we had a lovely time,
They ranx a bus to Rimini, through the Gothic Line,
Soon to Bologna we will go,
Where Jerry's gone beyond the Po,
For we're the D day dodgers out here in Italy.

Oh ? Lady Astor we know what you've got,
Don't stand on a platform and talk a lot of rot,
You're such a sweetheart, the nation's pride;
But tow us your mouth is far too wide,
That's from the D day lodger out here in Italy.

SOFTLY.

If you look around the mountains in the mud and rain,
You'll find the scattered crosses some which bear no name,
Heartbreak and toil and suffering gone,
The boys beneath them slumber on,
They were the D day dodgers out here in Italy.

-------O--------

PRESENTATION.

O-O-O- :- :-:-O-O
```

D-Day Dodgers song sheet taken from my farewell dinner.

lege in wartime to meet a large number of Indians, Sikhs, Gurkhas and so on. It baffles me that the government of the day should behave in such a difficult way over the Ghurkhas. They were very brave as their decorations have shown, apart from all the praise that has been heaped upon them. Those concerned should be welcomed wholeheartedly into this country. Thanks to Joanna Lumley and others this matter has been happily concluded whilst I write this book.

I would just like to refer to more recent times in the Services, particularly as regards the wars in Iraq and Afghanistan. As far as the troubles in Iraq are concerned I would mention that two of the many books that my father left me were large tomes of Gertrude Bell; these volumes set out how the state of Iraq was originally formed in the hope that warring tribes could live peacefully together. Having said that, the services have bravely done all their tasks and more in these difficult regions over the past years. Hopefully it will all end soon.

For many years I have had my haircut locally at Kew, and for many years the owner of this hairdressing establishment was Italian. It so happened he had a black and white picture hanging up in the salon of Cassino as it looked before World War II. I had for some time, when looking at this picture, tried to imagine how peaceful Cassino looked with the Monastery above in those days. I never did return to that area in more peaceful times, nor indeed to Point 593. On one occasion I did in fact obtain the details of Sergeant Hammett's grave in the Commonwealth Cemetery, but I had to cancel plans to visit at that time. It so happened that much later on a former business colleague of mine, Brian Henman, made a peacetime visit to this area and kindly sent me some impressive colour prints of the Monastery now in peace time.

It is strange that while I write this book there is quite a loud noise being made in the media about MPs and their own interpretation of expenses allowances, to their advantage of course! It reminds me in a way of my experience with post war credits.

These were savings that were taken from the Forces in wartime as part of the war effort on the condition that they would be given back to individuals after the war. For many years the government of the day shelved this matter in spite of some of us badgering them to give us back our due. Eventually I wrote a letter to Dick Taverne MP who I seem to remember was an Independent at that time. At last I had a sympathetic ear and the day came when I received the rebate. Sadly of course, the amount I received back did not account for the way the value of the £ had altered since those wartime days!

Of course the wartime government was not particularly sensitive to what mail we received in the midst of battle, although the mail home was rightly censored. Try to imagine receiving some mail from the UK when your distance from the enemy is only a cricket pitch length away, then imagine one of the envelopes you open is from the Inland Revenue about your taxes! Well that happened to me! When I reflect on the memories of those long ago grim days I suppose you could say that in the post war years I kept in touch at reunions with the likes of Ben Dalton; he could wriggle his ears, not one of my accomplishments! Also I could often recall the likes of Peter Cavalier, John Buckeridge, Jack Glennie, Goldie (Goldsmith), Bob Lumley, Len Mansfield, Pluto (Plutheroe) and Tommy Gardner and others. I had also met Len Mansfield's family over the years and his recent sad loss was a great loss to his family and friends.

There were those chance meetings too after the war. One day I was travelling to work on a crowded commuter train in London. Although I had a seat there were a considerable number of passengers strap hanging. As I looked up from my newspaper I caught the eye of Bruno Bryant who was standing further down the carriage. He had been my first Company Commander in North Africa. It's a pity we cannot spend a few minutes together because of the crowd I thought. I went back to reading the newspaper but suddenly Bruno appeared, he had made a point of struggling through the crowd to have a chat. I think it is right to say that when you have been through a common danger like war, then friendship never weakens. There was an occasion when I met someone by the name of Malpas briefly. As it so happens the chance meeting was outside the Ritz and he had been a very efficient person in charge of various messes.

Perhaps one of the strangest chance meetings I experienced was in Notting Hill Gate a few years after the war. He and his wife had passed me in the street and then we both turned around; it was Alan Plutheroe and his wife. He had been our company clerk and then he was promoted to Orderly Room Sergeant before leaving the army. We kept in touch, meeting from time to time for lunch. He also met Ben Dalton more recently as they lived in the same part of Surrey. Then there was the member of the Tube staff whose name I cannot remember! He told me to look after myself!

Sadly of course, many of these names are no longer with us, including Ben Clegg, who had been in charge of Patrol Courses in Palestine which I attended. I would also like to refer to Bob Lumley who had been a young Platoon Commander in the earlier days. When he left the army he resided in Cambridgeshire. We usually met at annual reunions in London and after the function we would adjourn to a nearby hostelry for a final beer. I'm sure he liked these occasions before he went home to rejoin his wife and children. Then one day I received news that he had been killed in a road accident. To think that he had come through all that war in the infantry without a scratch, and now he had left his young family. Jack Glennie phoned me to know if I had any further details, but I did not know what had actually happened; I still don't. I believe his grave is embellished with the Royal Sussex Cap Badge outline. I sincerely hope that his young family were looked after at the time.

I did attend the service at Westminster Abbey to mark the 50th anniversary of the battles of Monte Cassino in May 1944.

In Westminster Abbey they keep a Regimental Roll of Honour of the Queen's Westminsters; you will recall that this was the Regiment I joined in the dark days in 1939 before war was declared. Apparently in the Abbey they turn a page every day of this Roll of Honour. Sadly the two chaps who persuaded me to join this Regiment at that time did not survive the war as far as I know. Their names were Miller and Everitt and I never did meet them again.

To end on a lighter note, usually in those far off days if you had a jeep at your disposal on active service, you had a jeep driver as well. After the war was over, I think it was at the time when I and my Company were stationed at Ulm, I decided one day to drive myself for a while. All was going well until one of my large army boots caught under a pedal. It seemed to me that I was then heading at speed straight for the Danube. I managed to correct matters at the last seconds. The jeep driver (alas not Pantry who was no longer with us then) politely turned to me and said, "Would you like me to drive now Sir?"